BLACK AND BLUE

Black and Blue

Jazz Stories

STANLEY PÉAN

TRANSLATED BY DAVID HOMEL

Véhicule Press

Published with the generous assistance of the Canada Council for the Arts, the Canada Book Fund of the Department of Canadian Heritage, and the Société de développement des entreprises culturelles du Québec (SODEC).

Canada 🍁 SODEC Québec 🏵🏵

 Canada Council   Conseil des arts
for the Arts   du Canada

Cover design by David Drummond
Set in Adobe Minion and Bodoni MT by Simon Garamond
Printed by Livres Rapido Books

Originally published as *De préférence la nuit*
by Les Éditions du Boréal copyright © 2019
English translation copyright © David Homel 2022

Dépôt légal, Library and Archives Canada and the
Bibliothèque national du Québec, third trimester 2022

LIBRARY AND ARCHIVES CANADA CATALOGUING IN PUBLICATION

Title: Black and blue : jazz stories / Stanley Péan ; translated by David Homel.
Other titles: De préférence la nuit. English
Names: Péan, Stanley, 1966- author.
Description: Translation of: De préférence la nuit.
Identifiers: Canadiana (print) 20220262950 | Canadiana (ebook) 20220263051 | ISBN 9781550656114
(softcover) | ISBN 9781550656176 (HTML)
Subjects: LCSH: Jazz—History and criticism. | LCSH: Jazz musicians—Biography. | lcgft: Biographies.
Classification: LCC ML3506 P4313 2022 | DDC 781.65—dc23

Published by Véhicule Press, Montréal, Québec, Canada

Distribution in Canada by LitDistCo
www.litdistco.ca

Distribution in the U.S. by Independent Publishers Group
ipgbook.com

Printed in Canada on FSC certified paper.

For you, hidden in every line,
in the margins and between the words
though you will never read them

CONTENTS

Very nice. But can you tell me a story?

[Lester Young to a young sax player who had tried to impress him with a virtuoso display of be-bop lines]

What did I do to be so black and blue?

[Fats Waller, 1929, as immortalized by Louis Armstrong]

What Is this Thing Called Jazz?

In the magnificent film by the Italian Giuseppe Tornatore, *The Legend of 1900*, there is a particularly compelling scene that I like to point to when someone asks me what jazz is.

We are in the days of the Great Depression. At the foot of the majestic ocean liner, *The Virginian*, which is tied up in a port, a line of poor folks is waiting in front of a makeshift hiring desk. Sitting behind it, a man in a bowler hat is interviewing potential candidates for the crew. Played by Pruitt Taylor Vince, Max Tooney (known as Tim in Alessandro Baricco's story that inspired the film) sets down an instrument case in front of the man.

"What do you do?"

"I play the trumpet."

"We've already got musicians on board. Next!"

With the courage born of despair, Max pulls out his instrument and raises it to his lips. To the hiring agent's amazement, he launches into a heart-stopping improvisation in all the colors of blue, a spontaneous lament that carries his hopes and dreams, his pleasures and pain, his enthusiasm and unhealed wounds. Still playing, he starts marching, and his virtuoso, flamboyant blues take on depth and breadth. The music attracts a crowd, and Max keeps on blowing as if his life depends on it. Who knows? Maybe it really does.

When he finally draws his lips from the embouchure, the crowd goes wild. The man in the top hat, won over, asks him a simple question.

"What was that?"

"I don't know," Max Tooney admits.

"When you don't know what it is, it's jazz! Jazz, I say!"

Alessandro Baricco wrote the theatrical monologue *Novecento* on which Giuseppe Tornatore based his film. Baricco ended his preface to *The Soul of Hegel and the Cows of Wisconsin*, his essay on the shock of modernity in music, with the classic definition of jazz attributed to Louis Armstrong: "If you have to ask what jazz is, you'll never know."

Armstrong, the New Orleans trumpet player and singer, and one of the leading figures of the art, was not very inclined to discourse about the form. Yet, over his career, he did provide some useful hints to that never-ending question asked by Cole Porter: "What is this thing called jazz?"

Useful, also, is this tautology that Armstrong offered with his usual joking demeanor: "Jazz is what I point my finger at when I say: 'This is jazz.'"

On the subject of teasing rejoinders, try out this one. When a journalist asked Old Satchmo with some disdain whether jazz was a form of folk music, he answered, "Man, all music is folk music. You ain't never heard no horse sing a song, have you?"

We could head over to the fifth edition of Webster's Collegiate Dictionary from 1936 and read, "A type of American music, characterized by melodious themes, subtly syncopated dance rhythms and varied orchestral coloring." Or travel to New York, to the Jazz Workshop, and hear that "the key elements of Jazz include blues, syncopation, swing and creative freedom. Improvisation in music is not new as there are traditions of improvisation in India, Africa and Asia. Beethoven, Mozart and Bach all improvised, as well, but Jazz improvisation is special due to the use of the blues scale. The blues scale has a universal appeal that reached the core of emotional satisfaction."

Now, these definitions might be quite precise and almost scholarly, but in my opinion they don't succeed in getting across the liveliness and expressiveness we associate with this music of the senses and the essences, a music of spontaneous creation, as visceral as it is dreamy and refined.

I have been passionate about blue notes since the end of my teenage years, and ever since then I have marveled over the magnificent voyage of this supposed "folk music." From the streets and bordellos of New Orleans to the classrooms of the most prestigious conservatories, with a stop in the smoky nightclubs of Paris and the most illustrious concert halls of the world's capitals, in less than a century, jazz has proved itself to be the soundtrack of a century rich in leaps forward and disturbances of all kinds.

I don't quite know how to react when a stranger confesses, sometimes with regret, other times with arrogant pride, to an aversion for jazz. You don't like jazz, really? But what jazz are you talking about? The field is so vast, and so varied. Do you mean Armstrong's banter, Ellington's elegance, Billie's spleen, Ella's joie de vivre – which one bothers you? Is it Django's dexterity, Bird's flight, Miles' falsely prudish sobriety, Trane's mystical trances, or Ayler's fury that aggravates your delicate eardrums? Please, do tell me...

This book is not out to dissect and define the many esthetics of jazz, nor convince anyone of their value. I am interested in what people say about the music, and in some of its most illustrious artists, and its representation in other works of art, be they movies, novels, or plays. (Cole Porter is the only exception here. He is a writer and composer of pop-ular songs, not a jazz musician properly speaking, but he has contributed enough standards to the repertory that I consider him worthy of a place in these pages.)

Miles Davis, like his big brother Louis Armstrong, was not the kind of man to theorize. When asked, he would answer, "Don't write about the music, man. The music speaks for itself."

Yet I am about to do just that... as a way of letting us go back to the music and listen with more educated ears.

Suffer in Rhythm

They say we are better off not revisiting our old flames. Beware of exposing yourself to the pain. As my best friends keep telling me, there is something vaguely morbid about the way I so often yield to that temptation.

Is that why I had not opened my copy of the novel *Nausea* since I first discovered it as a literature student? Not exactly. You see, I had a bone to pick with Jean-Paul Sartre, especially after reading *Mémoires d'une jeune fille dérangée* (*A Disgraceful Affair*) by Bianca Lamblin, first published in 1993. Lamblin was born Bianca Bienenfeld in 1921 in Poland, a country her parents fled because of the stink of anti-Semitism that would not leave the air. The title itself is a parody of Simone de Beauvoir's *Jeune fille rangée* (*Memoirs of a Dutiful Daughter*). Lamblin had a *ménage à trois* with Beauvoir, who was her teacher, and Sartre, and she easily recognized herself in the character of Louise Védrine, the pseudonym Beauvoir gave her in her book *Lettres au Castor et à quelques autres*, a collection of her correspondence.

Insulted by what Beauvoir said about her in letters published from the 1980s onward, Lamblin, a philosophy professor, wrote her own memoir to set the record straight about the star couple of Paris' Left Bank a half a century earlier. Needless to say, her portrait of Sartre and Beauvoir would have been at home in Dorian Gray's closet.

Since I read this disturbing book, I have pretty much accepted that we have to separate the work, especially the greatest ones, from the artists who created them for us. The work has to be held above the fray, and we will leave the moralists to judge the artists' behavior when it comes to common human decency. Whatever the case, I've had a misunderstanding with Sartre since I was in my mid-twenties because of all the inglorious anecdotes attached to him and because of his quarrels with Camus, who is still closest to my heart. I am using the word *misunderstanding* on purpose in memory of the homage given by the author of *Being and Nothingness* to his ex-friend, the day after his death. Speaking of the late Albert Camus, Sartre wrote:

> He and I had a misunderstanding. A misunderstanding is nothing – unless you never see each other again – it's just another way of living together without losing track of one another in the small, narrow world that is given us.

Thinking back to Sartre's reflections on the old jazz standard that serves as a leitmotif in *Nausea*, I resumed my relationship with him. I remembered those parts of the novel where the hero and narrator, Antoine Roquentin, contrasts the time of our existence with that of the arts, especially music, which in this book happens to be jazz. With a smile, I recalled that Duke Ellington entitled one of his compositions "Melancholia," which was the working title of Sartre's novel. He had chosen it as a reference to Albrecht Dürer's engraving of the same name, but his publisher Gaston Gallimard wanted the title replaced.

Let's go back to *Nausea*'s plot and subject matter. Unmarried, in his thirties, Antoine Roquentin is living off his inheritance in the fictional town of Bouville. Weary of traveling and the idea he once had of adventure, he abandoned a career that took him to North Africa, central Europe, and the Far East. Now he is spending most of his time writing the biography of the Marquis de Rollebon, an aristocrat from the end of the eighteenth century – another of Sartre's fictional characters – while keeping a journal that will become the novel. As the days go by, he begins to experience an odd malaise and notices that his relationship with ordinary objects is changing. Everything seems slightly unpleasant to him, and he begins to fall into a state of persistent Nausea (the capital letter is Sartre's). When he experiences one of numerous episodes, he cannot look upon himself without feeling a deep disgust. One of the initial and most intense episodes takes place in a park. Casting his eyes on the exposed roots of a chestnut tree, Roquentin finds that everything around him feels foreign: from the bourgeoisie of Bouville to which he belongs, to the Marquis who will soon become meaningless in his eyes.

Sitting at a table in the Rendez-vous des cheminots, a café where he is a regular, Antoine Roquentin's flattened existence is shaken by "Some of These Days," an old ragtime tune that he once heard American soldiers casually whistling. Sartre returns several times to the song and uses it to write a long meditation that fills the final pages of the novel. Along the way, he attributes authorship of it to a Brooklyn Jew sweating out a heat wave and dreaming of an old lover.

> The American with the black eyebrows sighs, gasps and the sweat rolls down his cheeks. He is sitting, in shirtsleeves, in front of his piano; he has a taste of smoke in his mouth and, vaguely, a ghost of a tune in his head. [...] "Some of these days." The moist hand seizes the pencil on the piano. "Some of these days you'll miss me, honey."
>
> That's the way it happened. That way or another way, it makes little difference. That is how it was born. It is the worn-out body of this Jew with black eyebrows which it chose to create it. (Translation: Robert Baldick)

But that's not the way it happened. Not at all. The wrongness of this fantasy scene did not strike the eager teenage reader I was when I first came across the book. But today I wonder why Sartre made a New York Jew out of Shelton Brooks, a Black writer and composer from Amherstburg, Ontario. Brooks doesn't have a Hebrew bone in his body, though he is the author of any number of successful tunes, including "The Darktown Strutters' Ball," "I Wonder Where My Easy Rider's Gone," "Every Day," "All Night Long," "Somewhere in France," "Swing That Thing," "That Man of Mine," "There'll Come a Time," as well as his celebrated "Walkin' the Dog" that has nothing to do with George Gershwin's composition of the same name, nor with Rufus Thomas' R & B hit appropriated by the Rolling Stones at a much later date.

In Chicago, where his parents settled when he was a teenager, Brooks, who was Afro but not yet Canadian, was making a living as a ragtime piano player and imitator before springing full-fledged into his identity as a songwriter-composer with his very first tune. According to legend, in 1910, he was walking the streets of the Windy City, pursued by a ragtime melody in a minor key, though he couldn't find the right words to go with it. Sitting in a diner one day, he overheard a turbulent conversation between a Black couple at a nearby table. "Some of these days, you'll miss me, honey," the woman warned her boyfriend, putting him on notice not to even think of leaving her for someone else.

Brooks was struck dumb. He realized immediately that the words went perfectly with his melody. After this first element that set everything into motion, the rest of the lyrics practically wrote themselves. His song finished, Brooks apparently offered it to a popular lady singer who, according to Noble Sissle and Eubie Blake, was in the habit of supporting the works of young, aspiring Black composers. His hunch was excellent, since the very next day, the singer in question made the piece part of her repertoire, and it would become her signature song for the next half-century.

Not exactly the scene as imagined by Roquentin.

Just as Sartre and his alter ego presumed that the writer was a Brooklyn Jew, not an African Canadian, they assumed that the voice that echoed in their ears was necessarily that of a Black woman. I'm willing to bet that around 1933, the time he was writing *Nausea*, Sartre did not know of two young singers named Billie Holiday and Ella Fitzgerald."

In any case, they didn't record the song until 1956 and 1970, respectively. As for Ma Rainey and Bessie Smith, the two most famous Black vocalists of the time, who most re-semble the fantasy singer imagined by Roquentin, they never recorded "Some of These Days."

As a matter of fact, the only African Americans who did so at the time were Evelyn Preer, the first Black screen actress, singing with pianist Fletcher Henderson's orchestra, back in January 1927 for the Vocalion label. That same year, Ethel Waters recorded her version for Black Swan. The two 78s are extremely rare, and Sartre obviously never got near them.

Most sources agree that the arrangement described in *Nausea* belongs to the singer of "Some of These Days," Sophie Tucker, accompanied by clarinetist Ted Lewis' orchestra in 1926. This version, which wasn't Tucker's first, but is considered today as the classic one, sold a million copies and sat at the top of the charts for five straight weeks starting on November 23 of that year.

Tucker, a zaftig, fire-breathing Jew of Ukrainian roots, who was born Sonya Kalish, was an enormously popular actress and singer in the United States during the first half of the twentieth century. Not only did audiences watch her perform "Some of These Days" on the big screen in *Honky Tonk* (1929), *Broadway Melody of 1938* (1937), and *Follow the Boys* (1944), but her career was so strongly associated with the song that she used its title for her autobiography published in 1945.

To be fair to Sartre, the Last of the Red Hot Mamas, like many performers on the vaudeville circuit of the time, made her debut in 1907 in theaters whose directors recommended her to darken her face with burnt cork and put on a Deep South accent. But Roquentin could not have picked that up from listening to a record. It so happened that, two years into her long career, Tucker lost her makeup case during a tour one day. The corpulent Sophie went on stage *au naturel* and spoke these words to her audience:

> You-all can see I'm a white girl. Well, I'll tell you something more: I'm not Southern. I'm a Jewish girl and I just learned this Southern accent doing a blackface act for two years. And now, Mr. Leader, please play my song.

When I think about it, it's an amusing paradox that Jean-Paul Sartre and his fictional double imagined a Jewish songwriter-composer and a Black woman singer – the exact opposite of reality. In his recent book *Some of These Days: Black Stars, Jazz Aesthetics, and Modernist Culture*, critic James Donald considers this mix-up a simple anecdote with no great meaning, an indulgent point of view that I respect but do not share.

That being said, let's go back to the song, what it states and what it implies.

> *Some of these days, you'll miss me, honey*
> *Some of these days, you're gonna be so lonely*
> *You'll miss my huggin', you're gonna miss my kissin'*
> *You're gonna miss me, honey, when I'm far away*

I've had more than my share of this kind of experience, so I can easily imagine, though it is painful to do so, the domestic farce that inspired these lines. The warning with its underlying threat carries a whiff of megalomania. When you love with a passion, you believe you're irreplaceable. Both sides are happy to bathe in that gratifying illusion. And if you believe, wrong-headed as it is, that the other person couldn't possibly go on living if you broke up, if you wish for that secretly just a little, it's because the contrary seems unconceivable. That's because the idea leaves us with the bitter impression that the affair that is about to end was actually less grand, less spectacular, less absolute than we would have wanted. After me, not the deluge, but emptiness – so believes the disconsolate and inconsolable lover. Obviously, such a person would not find shelter with Sartre, but would be better off with Ionesco, who staged an egocentric sovereign whose kingdom literally falls apart as he descends toward death and disappears with him.

~

"Some of These Days" is not the first and won't be the last number in the Great American Songbook to express that point of view about love's demise. Without having to dig too deep, I thought of "After You've Gone," lyrics by Henry Creamer and music by Turner Layton, a song created in 1918 by Marion Harris and also sung by Sophie Tucker in 1927. Then there's "Someday You'll Be Sorry," words and music by Louis Armstrong at the end of the 1920s, wherein the rejected lover (or friend) warns the other party that she (or he…) will regret breaking off the affair. I also considered Arthur Hamilton's "Cry Me a River," first written for Ella Fitzgerald, but created and immortalized by Julie London in 1955, a song in which the scorned woman insists that the flighty lover who now wants to come back to her first prove his love and sincerity by crying a river.

I thought of "Who's Sorry Now?" by Ted Snyder, Bert Kalmar, and Harry Ruby. I first heard Nat King Cole's elegant version, backed by Billy May's orchestra, in the King's desert island compilation of breakup songs entitled *Just One of Those Things* (Capitol, 1957). In the song, made into a rock 'n' roll megahit in 1958 by Connie Francis, the rejected lover licks his chops over the subsequent heartbreaks of the woman who made him suffer.

Along the same lines, I could point to "You're Gonna Miss Me," written and composed by Eddie Curtis in 1959 expressly for Connie Francis. Then there's "You're Gonna Miss Me When I'm Gone" by John Lee Hooker, the master of stinging blues guitar chords. The man had a way of stating his refrains with murderous intent.

Returning to melancholy, we should not forget "You Won't Forget Me," that Joan Crawford lip-synched on the big screen in *Torch Song* (1953). Today we know that a certain India Adams lent the star her voice. The tune fell out of favor until 1990, when pianist and singer Shirley Horn turned it into a blues summit meeting with her guardian angel, Miles Davis. The two authors, Fred Spielman and Kermit Goell, used the terms of melancholy to express the conviction that, even in the arms of a new flame, the lover will never erase the memory of the moments with the one who was left behind: *I'm part of memories too wonderful to die...*

In the same vein, take "I'll Be Around," written and composed by Alec Wilder in 1942. Another contemporary singer, Chaka Khan, turned to Miles Davis' spleen-tinged trumpet phrasings in 1987. Of all the versions I know (from Mildred Bailey's original to follow-ups from Rebecca Kilgore, Helen Merrill, Doris Day, Peggy Lee, Tony Bennett, Frank Sinatra, and many more), none measures up to Billie Holiday's. Hers speaks eloquently of the endless pain of the woman left behind who promises to be there to console her lost lover once his new flame leaves him. Despite the sugary flight of the violins of Ray Ellis' orchestra that accompany her on *Lady in Satin* (1958), Billie knows better than anyone else the meaning of Sartre's words in *Nausea*: "suffer in rhythm."

Who could forget the more vengeful, "I Wanna Be Around," in which the rejected lover states his dishonorable desire to be in the front row to watch his former beloved being shown the door, the day her new man decides to drop her. The song's genesis merits a few words. Inspired by the conjugal crisscross of Frank Sinatra – who had just divorced his wife Nancy to flit off with Ava Gardner, who would soon leave him in the lurch – in 1957 an Ohio housewife by the name of Sadie Vimmerstedt wrote the first line of the lyrics ("I wanna be around to pick up the pieces when somebody breaks your heart"), intending to send her contribution to Johnny Mercer. Since she didn't have the songwriter-composer's address, the lady sent the envelope to "Johnny

Mercer… Songwriter… New York, NY." Fortunately for her, a postal worker had the bright idea of forwarding the letter to the offices of the American Society of Composers, Authors, and Publishers (ASCAP). Not only did an impressed Mercer write the rest of the words and the music in 1959, picking up on the thread offered by Mrs. Vimmerstedt, he credited her as the co-author and gave her a third of the writing royalties for the song that Tony Bennett turned into a smash hit in 1963.

Though nothing indicates that Sinatra was aware of his role in the birth of "I Wanna Be Around," I think it's ironic that he recorded it in 1964 on his album *It Might as Well Be Spring*, backed by the Count Basie orchestra.

Like Francis Bacon said, revenge is a kind of wild justice.

∾

The reference in *Nausea* to "Some of These Days" and its subject, which is the future pain that one person will feel at the departure of the other, is no accident. Not when you consider the character of Anny, Roquentin's former lover whom he thinks of from time to time with a touch of melancholy. He receives a letter from her, asking him to meet her in a Paris hotel, and this throws him back to his memories of their past. "What does she want? I have no idea," the narrator wonders. The reunion with Anny, four years after their breakup, gives rise to a rather theatrical scene. The atmosphere is tense, and though at first he is happy to see her again, Roquentin soon feels ill at ease. The conversation quickly turns to accusations and reveals the wounds that have never healed.

He understands this hard and fast truth: it is better to avoid revisiting past loves. Then comes a sense of resignation. He thought he would come back to her, but now he must leave her again. Suddenly she seems much less desirable to him, as if she had turned into an old woman before his eyes. Maybe as a result of his cruelty, she laughs at him and kicks him out: "Poor boy! He never has any luck. The first time he plays his part well, he gets no thanks for it."

This scene sums up the theme of the novel. Long before Roquentin does, Anny seems to understand that existence itself is incomplete. Thirsting for absolutes, she searches for "perfect moments," "situations which had a rare and precious quality, style, if you like." Love for her is a brief and mediocre transcendence, "the infinite placed within the reach of poodles," as another French writer, Louis-Ferdinand Céline, put it.

Once this scene is over, Roquentin knows he will never see Anny again. Yet the next day he crosses paths with her at the station. They don't speak to each other, and he takes his appointed train. Am I projecting too far to imagine him, some time later, casting out part of the pain of this final encounter to the sound of "Some of These Days," picturing himself for a brief moment in the skin of this Brooklyn Jew whose real identity was Shelton Brooks?

Roquentin contemplates him from afar, in a July heat wave.

I try to think of him through the melody, through the white, acidulated sounds of the saxophone. [...] There is nothing pretty or glorious in all that. But when I hear the sound and I think that that man made it, I find this suffering and sweat ... moving. He was lucky. He couldn't have realized it. (Translation: Robert Baldick)

Coming from Roquentin, the perfect misanthrope, those comments are surprising. He ends with a confession, almost fraternal, that "I'd like to know something about him. It would interest me to find out the type of troubles he had." With a woman, probably. Sartre's narrator seems to have found a mirror, but he won't look upon his reflection. "Some of these days, you'll miss me, Anny," he might have sung.

"I wanna be around to pick up the pieces when somebody breaks your heart," he could have added, as Sinatra did a quarter-century later.

Sartre and his character Roquentin are less concerned with the delightful certainty that their ex will suffer as much as they did. What touches them is the staging of pain that they expect, and anticipate, and even wish for.

It seems inevitable, so strong is the necessity of this music: nothing can interrupt it, nothing which comes from this time in which the world has fallen; it will stop of itself, as if by order. If I love this beautiful voice it is especially because of that: it is neither for its fullness nor its sadness, rather because it is the event for which so many notes have been preparing, from so far away, dying that it might be born.

After the final chord fades, in the silence that follows, Roquentin realizes that his Nausea has disappeared. That is the surprise discovery he makes at the very end of the novel. Until then, he is quick to point out that works of art, especially music, exist only to turn the attention of fools away from the vicissitudes of existence, to ease the passage of time, as Borges liked to say. Until then, all attempts to sidestep the human condition that way are pure complacency in Roquentin's opinion.

His contact with two sculptures (the Khmer statuette he contemplates at the beginning of the novel and the arrogant statue of the writer Gustave Impétraz sporting a top hat in the library courtyard, like the Commander in Don Juan), the presence of works of art, and the materiality of bronze and stone serve only to communicate the nauseating sensation of the inevitable decay of the human body, the final degradation of existence. As for music and songs, what more can be said beyond this old chestnut that fits so well here: "Long after the poets have disappeared, their songs will be still heard in the streets…"

Though jazz standards are open to interpretation, the one that Roquentin is obsessed with has the solidity of a "steel ribbon" and an implacable tempo, as imposing as bronze or stone. The notes played by an orchestra as ordinary as Ted Lewis' (a clarinetist of limited means if ever there was one) and the words sung by the fake "Negress" Sophie Tucker follow "an inflexible order."

Maybe Sartre the novelist paid no attention to the lyrics of "Some of These Days," and made the choice completely by accident. The standard could simply be an element of the sound design, unlike some books that are full of references to contemporary musical works that create atmospheres and establish connections with the reader. Still other writers will display their erudition by trying to add density and credibility to their works that, otherwise, they would not have.

Like film in *The Words*, an autobiographical memoir that some observers think is Sartre's answer to Camus' *The Fall*, art in *Nausea* serves as a revealer. Whether cinema or music, works of art show their value because everything in them is indispensable, and everything has a reason for being there, whereas so-called reality is composed of heterogeneous elements without necessity.

And so the epiphany, these words, in the final pages of the novel that Sartre presents as an apologue of Roquentin's experience: "You must be like me; you must suffer in rhythm."

In a Mist

The scene looks like something straight out of a Grade-B Hollywood movie. Imagine an apartment block in Queen's, New York City, on a torrid August evening in 1931. The camera zeros in: the action takes place in Sunnyside, at 43-30 46th Street. The tenant from 1G bursts into the lobby, screaming for the man who rented him the place, a certain George Kraslow. The son of a building contractor, Kraslow shows up promptly. He likes conversing and sipping gin with the occupant of that apartment, a recent arrival in the building.

Until a short time ago, the guy made his living playing cornet in a popular band. Scarcely older than George, the musician always has the same pretty woman on his arm, who was prone to complain because of his drunkenness. According to her, George is one of the few people that the musician trusts, and the woman wants him to convince her man to cut down on his alcohol intake. George is a little worried, too, and some evenings he even hides the gin bottle. But the musician isn't above begging, and he always ends up getting George to hand over the bottle, which he immediately empties.

George has had to field the neighbors' complaints.

Sometimes the voice of the cornet wakes them up in the bluest hour of the night, but they are so moved by the music that they don't make a formal complaint, and neither do they want George to discourage his friend. The routine has been going on for weeks now, but tonight, George senses that the worst is at hand. "His hysterical screams brought me to his apartment on the run," he would relate, a quarter-century later, to one of the biographers of his tenant who had become a legend in the meantime.

> "He pulled me in and pointed to the bed. His whole body was trembling violently. He was screaming that there were two Mexicans hiding under the bed with long knives. To humor him, I looked under the bed and when I rose to assure him that there was no one hiding there, he staggered and fell, a dead weight, in my arms. I ran across the hall and called in a woman doctor, Dr. Haberski, to examine him. She pronounced him dead."

No doubt about it, the scene would have been perfectly at home in a low-budget melodrama. But it is not to be found in either of the two major films inspired by the tragic, tumultuous, and brief life of Leon Bismark Beiderbecke, better known by the diminutive "Bix." Today, there is still some dissension among jazz historians as to the identity of the doctor who signed the death certificate, but the diagnosis was unquestionable. Bix Beiderbecke, Louis Armstrong's only serious rival (the uncontested "sun king" of the early years of jazz) and the star soloist of Paul

Whiteman's symphonic jazz orchestra (the self-proclaimed king of jazz of the Roaring Twenties) died of pneumonia as a result of alcohol abuse.

His body was brought back to his hometown of Davenport, Iowa, by his brother Burnie and his mother and buried there five days later. His premature death at age 28 turned the cornetist, who up until then was recognized only by jazz aficionados, into a kind of romantic hero. His life would become emblematic of the traditional conflict between art and the everyday constraints that keep it from fully flowering, from family to the laws of the marketplace. In his book *Remembering Bix: A Memoir of the Jazz Age*, Ralph Berton goes as far as comparing him to Jesus Christ. A martyr in spite of himself, Beiderbecke would become the "First Saint" in the history of jazz, according to the sarcastic formulation in *The Reluctant Art: Five Studies in the Growth of Jazz* by the critic and British saxophonist Benny Green. He should not be confused with his contemporary, the American trombone player Bennie Green, nor with our contemporary and disciple of Oscar Peterson, the pianist Benny Green. It feels like I've just stumbled into that scene from Ionesco's *Bald Soprano* where suddenly everyone is named Bobby Watson.

∾

Like in a black-and-white movie, let's fade into a smoky flashback, in a mist. Imagine a wide shot of Davenport, Iowa, on the shores of the Mississippi, east of Des Moines and west of Chicago. The town was established in 1836 by the Métis Antoine LeClaire, who named the place after Colonel

George Davenport who put up the first buildings on the site. In 1856, Davenport would witness the completion of the inaugural railroad bridge over Ol' Man River, much to the chagrin of the steamboat industry, which feared for its revenue stream. A few weeks after the bridge was christened, the captain of the *Effie Afton* deliberately plowed into the bridge, giving its owner the perfect pretext to sue the Rock Island Line. The trial would feature a battle between rail and river transport, with the defense hiring the services of a young lawyer named Abraham Lincoln.

But the story that concerns us begins in early spring of 1903. The son of German immigrants, a self-made man grown prosperous dealing in roofing timber and coal, Bismark Herman Beiderbecke was awaiting the birth of his third child. His wife, Agatha Jane Beiderbecke, née Hilton, was the daughter of a steamboat captain. This second son would see the light of day on March 10, eight years after his older brother Charles Burnette and five years after his sister Mary Louise. He would be baptized Leon Bismark Beiderbecke, but everyone, including the boy himself, preferred the affectionate nickname "Bix." Encouraged by his mother, who played organ in the town's Presbyterian church, the youngest Beiderbecke began playing piano at age two or three, as his sister remembered, standing in front of the instrument on his tiptoes to reach the keyboard, his arms outstretched above his head.

At the age of ten, if his brother Burnie is to be believed, young Bix would run down to the port after school in hopes of slipping onto one of the excursion boats. The crew would let him sit down at the calliope and play the melodies from the soundtracks for the silent films he watched on Saturday mornings. He would hear them once and then be able to reproduce them by heart. Another of Burnie's memories: in 1918, on his return from military service, he brought back a Victrola phonograph and a handful of records, including *Skeleton Jangle* and *Tiger Rag* by the Original Dixieland Jazz Band. Bix would listen endlessly to these hot jazz recordings, then reproduce on the cornet what Nick LaRocca played on the trumpet.

Strange but true: in their respective biographies, cornetist Louis Armstrong and drummer Baby Dodds both recall an encounter with the young Beiderbecke during a stop in Davenport, when they were performing on a riverboat in pianist Fate Marable's band. Alas, some historians are not convinced of the veracity of the anecdote. Whether it actually happened or not, Bix soon found his place at the opposite end of the stylistic spectrum from Satchmo. Both musicians are considered essential players, since they moved jazz from collective – the traditional New Orleans manner of playing – to individual improvisation, which would become the new and accepted way of conceiving of and interpreting the music.

New Orleans did produce some talented soloists, the most famous of them being the clarinetist Sidney Bechet, but in Ted Gioia's words in his *History of Jazz*, most of them "lacked the technical resources and, even more, the creative depth to make the solo into the compelling centerpiece of jazz music." With their first records in the middle of the 1920s, Armstrong and Beiderbecke would change the landscape, each according to his temperament. In *The*

Oxford Companion to Jazz, Digby Fairweather sets down what set them apart. Armstrong's playing was all bravura and openly emotional, whereas Beiderbecke's conveyed a range of intellectual alternatives. Where Armstrong, at the head of an ensemble, played it hard, straight, and true, Beiderbecke invented his own way of phrasing "around the lead." His cool approach invited rather than commanded you to listen.

Taking into account some small details, the stylistic opposition between Satchmo and Bix resembled what would differentiate Dizzy Gillespie from Miles Davis and Chet Baker. One side would put the accent on virtuoso performance, showmanship, and pyrotechnics, while the other would go for improvisation based on melodic extrapolation. But let's not get ahead of ourselves. Barely out of his teenage years, Bix was not yet the professional musician he was to become, influenced both by New Orleans hot jazz and the impressionism of Claude Debussy and Maurice Ravel. In the meantime, he played on and off for a variety of local bands. Then, in December 1920, after a complaint brought against him and some of his fellows who were not card-carrying members of the Guild, he was ordered to play an audition for a union representative. The representative refused to issue the card in question – Bix could not properly read a partition.

On April 22, 1921, just after his eighteenth birthday, he was charged with the kidnapping and sexual assault of a five-year-old girl. Though jailed briefly, Beiderbecke was freed because the girl could not provide unimpeachable evidence. According to her father's statement, she would have suffered further trauma had she been forced to describe her experiences in a court of law. This sordid incident resurfaced in 2005, in the late Jean Pierre Lion's definitive biography of Beiderbecke. But the book never declared whether the girl's father, in his statement, formally identified Bix as the person who assaulted his daughter.

Ashamed at being identified as a pedophile, Bix was sent by his parents to a boarding school in Lake Forest, Illinois, outside of Chicago. Historians disagree as to their motivations. Was it to cover up their son's arrest, or were they trying to discourage his musical ambitions by imposing a rigorous academic path on him? In any case, the young man's true interests never wavered. He often deserted the campus and slipped onto a train heading for Chicago to listen to jazz groups that played in the dives and speakeasies of the Windy City. His favorite haunt was the infamous Friar's Inn where, horn in hand, he sat in with the New Orleans Rhythm Kings, invited by Paul Mares, the band's cornet player. But that wasn't enough. He would explore the Black neighborhoods of the South Side in search of what he called the "real" musicians of hot jazz. "Don't think I'm getting hard, Burnie," Bix wrote to his older brother. "I'd go to hell to hear a good band."

With his colleague Walter "Cy" Welge, he cofounded a band at school. Bix attracted the administration's disapproval because of the immoral nature of the music they played at dances. That was only the beginning. He ignored the curfew and often did not return from his escapades until the next morning, which earned him more severe reprimands. Once he was caught trying to sneak back into the dormitory via the fire escape and expelled from the Lake Forest Academy. Not only were his grades poor, he drank to excess, including on campus, in clear violation of the rules.

Between the summer of 1922 and the fall of the following year, Bix made frequent trips to Chicago, where he began to make a name for himself as a musician. When he was back in Davenport, he worked at his father's business. At the end of 1923, he found himself in Hamilton, Ohio, playing in a hot jazz septet that was called the Wolverines, in honor of Jelly Roll Morton's "Wolverine Blues," the jewel of their repertoire. Around that time, his piano teacher introduced him to the work of Eastwood Lane, an American composer deeply influenced by the French impressionists, who would put his stamp on Beiderbecke's musical imagination. The influence was clear to see in his famous "In a Mist," the only one of his piano compositions he would record, at the end of his career.

In winter 1924, nearly two years before the first recordings that Louis Armstrong made as leader of his mythical Hot Five, the Wolverines cut a dozen or more pieces for Gennett Records of Richmond, Indiana. Among them, on February 18, was the historic version of "Jazz Me Blues" that revealed Beiderbecke's innovative approach as a genius improviser. On May 6, the septet immortalized "Riverboat Shuffle," composed expressly for the group by Hoagy Carmichael. He and Bix became friends, and their paths frequently crossed.

Bix left the Wolverines in October 1924, and the young man with a cornet played on and off with a Detroit orchestra led by pianist Jean Goldkette. Eddie King, the artistic director, hardly appreciated Beiderbecke's improv style that he considered incompatible with commercial success, no more than he could tolerate his inability to read the sheet music laid out before him. Bix was fired after a few weeks, but he convinced the group's musicians to gather in a studio on January 25, 1925, to record a version of the Original Dixieland Jazz Band's "Toddlin' Blues" under the name Bix and his Rhythm Jugglers. But the high point of the session was the recording of his own composition "Davenport Blues."

After going back to school at the University of Iowa, from which he was soon expelled for absenteeism and his participation in a barroom brawl, Beiderbecke got back in touch with Goldkette, whose group jazzed up the evening dances at a Michigan vacation spot. That's where Bix met saxophonist Frankie Trumbauer, though the latter was warned to stay clear. "Look out, he's trouble," people would say. "He drinks and you'll have a hard time handling him." Despite the inauspicious beginning, the two men soon became best friends and Trumbauer, though only two years older than Bix, became a father figure for him. When Trumbauer was putting together a new group for the Arcadia Ballroom in Saint Louis, as leader he asked Bix to join as cornetist. According to Jean Pierre Lion's biography, clarinetist Pee Wee Russell, also a member of the band, would say of his colleague, "He makes you play, whether you like it or not. But if you had the slightest talent, he'd have you playing better."

Meanwhile, on November 12, 1925, in Chicago, Louis Armstrong was writing an essential page of jazz's young history with the first session at the head of his Hot Five, along with pianist Lillian Armstrong (née Hardin), trombonist Kid Ory, clarinetist Johnny Dodds, and banjo player Johnny St. Cyr. When the day's work was done (three themes bearing Satchmo's signature or that of his wife Lili), the band made up of alumni from King Oliver's orchestra had radically transformed American popular music. It soon began to flow in a hybrid style, a mix of forms from New Orleans, Chicago, and New York. In three years, the Hot Five – this first version or the others that followed – would put Armstrong at the very pinnacle of the universe of jazz with his dazzling improvisations, but also his distinctive singing voice. His ascension had just begun…

Back with Goldkette's group at Detroit's Graystone Ballroom, Frankie Trumbauer and Bix Beiderbecke were part of a number of the band's recordings beginning in the spring of 1926. But they were especially active in New York, once warming up for Fletcher Henderson's orchestra at the Roseland Ballroom. The venue's management promoted the two-part program as a battle of the bands. The morning after a night of the hottest jazz in town, the newspapers crowned Goldkette's men the kings, much to the disgruntlement of Henderson's musicians. A humiliation, according to Rex Stewart, the first trumpet for the latter group. And indeed it was. Known for his saccharine, squeaky-clean recordings that almost never allowed Beiderbecke's talents as an improviser to come to the fore, Goldkette's band could not possibly outperform Henderson's, one of the most prestigious Black orchestras of the time, boasting soloists like Louis Armstrong and Coleman Hawkins.

Fortunately, Trumbauer, Beiderbecke, and their colleagues could still record music closer to their own aspirations, in their own way, under their own names. In February 1927, the saxophonist brought together his boys to lay down tracks that let the cornetist's genius shine through, among them the immortal "Trumbology," "Clarinet Marmalade," and the luminous "Singin' the Blues." In May, back in the studio under Trambauer's lead, Bix revisited Carmichael's "Riverboat Shuffle" and, with the leader, cosigned "For No Reason at All in C," for which he shifted between piano and cornet.

Unsurmountable financial difficulties forced Jean Goldkette to dissolve his orchestra in the fall of 1927, much to the glee of Paul Whiteman, who coveted its best elements for his own group. Whiteman proclaimed himself "the King of Jazz," but most of the time his performances featured a mediocre blend of symphonic melodies with a timid touch of jazz now and again. The difference between this entertainment and true jazz played by someone of Duke Ellington's stature is obvious to anyone who has ears. Ellington, piano-and-all-around maestro, took over from Fletcher Henderson's group as the house band at Harlem's famous Cotton Club on December 4, 1927, and his Friday concerts were broadcast on the nation's airwaves. From the beginning of his lengthy residence at the Cotton Club until it ended in June 1931, Ellington developed an innovative repertoire made of pieces designed for dancing, overtures, and transitions for radio play, all of which gave him the latitude to experiment with "jungle" sounds and unusual orchestral colors. His enormous contribution to the Harlem

Renaissance numbers hundreds of original works in less than four years, most of which have become standards.

Not bad for an ordinary Duke!

On the other hand, the so-called king Whiteman had one important feather in his cap. On February 12, 1924, at New York's Aeolian Hall, he created the premiere of George Gershwin's *Rhapsody in Blue*, in Ferde Grofé's orchestration. Whiteman was also behind the creation, with the composer in attendance, of Gershwin's *Concerto in F* for piano and orchestra, including a brief bit of Beiderbecke in the first ten measures. What was Bix doing in that slave ship led by a man *The New Yorker* described in 1926 as "a man flabby, virile, quick, coarse, untidy and sleek, with a hard core of shrewdness in an envelope of sentimentalism"? Let's not underestimate the attraction of financial security. A spot in one of the most popular orchestras of the period did ensure that. Our critic Benny Green is pitiless in his evaluation of this "mediocre vaudeville act" that we tolerate today "in the hope that here and there a Bixian fragment will redeem the mess." But the cornetist's colleagues stated that Beiderbecke did not feel strait-jacketed in that context and saw in it a chance to improve his musical education. In 1928, as a member of Whiteman's orchestra, Bix cut four tunes that went to the top of the charts, including the famous version of "Ol' Man River" with vocals by a young Bing Crosby. According to the crooner, another of his songs owed its success partly to Beiderbecke, and that was Hoagy Carmichael's "Stardust," whose refrain found its inspiration in a recurring phrase in Bix's solos on "Singin' the Blues" and "Jazz Me Blues."

Despite his achievements, Bix was beginning to feel the devastating effects of his massive alcohol consumption; he simply couldn't spend a moment away from the stuff. After a bout of delirium tremens during which he destroyed his hotel room, he decided to seek shelter at his parents' house for a recovery period that would last through the winter. Briefly back in the saddle during the summer of 1929, he returned to Davenport in September and was finally interned from October 14 to November 18 for detox at the Keeley Institute in Dwight, Illinois. During his convalescence, Whiteman kept an empty chair on stage in his honor.

Returning to New York at the end of January 1930, the once-great star soloist was by then playing only occasionally for Whiteman, who continued paying him despite his lengthening absences. He showed up again with his good friend Hoagy Carmichael on a new composition by the latter, "Georgia on my Mind," recorded in mid-September, with the writer-composer on vocals, Jack Teagarden on trombone, Bud Freeman on tenor sax, Jimmy Dorsey on clarinet and alto sax, Eddie Lang on guitar, and Joe Venuti on violin. Later interpreted by a who's who of jazz and popular music, from Louis Armstrong to Billie Holiday to Ray Charles who made it his signature tune, "Georgia on my Mind" would have its original version inducted into the Grammy Hall of Fame in March 2014.

The Great Depression had begun, and the once-flourishing music industry had slowed to a crawl. By then, Beiderbecke was making a living from a radio show, *The Camel Pleasure Hour*, on which Whiteman's orchestra performed.

Then came the day when the unthinkable occurred. October 8, 1930. Bix's limitless gift for improvisation failed. He stood up for his solo, and…

Nothing.

Not the slightest note.

Fired some time later, Bix spent the rest of the year in Davenport. In February 1931, he was back in New York and moved into 43-30 46th Street over the summer.

You know the rest of the story.

∾

Seven years after Beiderbecke died, Dorothy Baker, a California writer, borrowed something from her journalist friend Otis Ferguson. It was the title of an article he had published in *The New Republic* in July 1936: "Young Man with a Horn." The words became the title of her first novel. The book is considered by some commentators as the founding work for any number of novels inspired by jazz and jazz musicians. Her book is not exactly a fictionalized biography, but it is obvious to any reader interested in traditional jazz that Baker used Bix as her model for the character of the young trumpet player whom she called Rick Martin – not to be confused with the Puerto Rican salsa king Ricky Martin. It looks as though we're falling back into that Ionesco play again…

Set in the universe of big bands and speakeasies at the time of the Harlem Renaissance, *Young Man with a Horn* tells the story of Rick Martin, a brilliant yet tormented musician, from his years as a young prodigy to his premature death at the age of 30. In a style as precise as her hero's trumpet phrasings, Baker brings us inside the mind of this young white man whose obsessive quest for excellence will inspire him to conquer the many obstacles in his way. And there are more than a few. He is an orphan with little patience for school and so poor he can't afford an instrument. Moved by forces beyond his understanding, Rick Martin plays hooky to teach himself piano at the local Black church. Soon he dreams of switching over to the trumpet, realizing that good luck and hard work will make it possible for him to buy one of the models in the pawnshop window. Working in a bowling alley, he meets Smoke Jordan, an 18-year-old Black youth whose job is to sweep the floor of the joint as he dances to the rhythm of his inner music.

United by their love of jazz, Smoke and Rick become inseparable, and this interracial friendship – an echo of the feelings between the runaway slave Jim and Huck in Mark Twain's *Huckleberry Finn* – is one of the novel's strong points. Like her contemporary Dorothy Parker (with whom she all but shared a name) in stories like "Arrangement in Black and White," "Big Blonde," and "The Standard of Living," Baker displays an exceptional understanding of the forces involved in class and race in post-slavery America, still traumatized by the wounds of the Civil War.

Even before he reaches legal age, Rick heads for New York and begins supporting himself with his music. In the Mecca of jazz, life proves complicated. In these pages, Baker taps into the dramatic potential of the conflicts between her hero's private life and his artistic aspirations. I am not the first to praise the way Dorothy Baker makes the reader feel the inner torment of a young artist, the way he invests body and soul in the simplest melodies in order to transform them and give them a greater dimension than just entertainment, aspiring to something universal. With a remarkably sober style, Baker makes the universe of creativity accessible to the readers we are. Through her, we come to grasp how jazzmen and women follow their muse to reach that moment, precious and rare, when inspiration reaches its highest point. And also the way those moments are different each time, with each interpretation of the same piece.

With her empathetic point of view, Baker portrays the obsessive search for the perfect note, the balanced arrangement, despite fatigue and the accidents of existence. To ward off melancholy and escape the constraints of the outside world, like Bix, Rick Martin will turn to alcohol ever more frequently, on stage and off. The goal: to live in a permanent state of stimulation and continue the endless quest for "perfect moments." Without moralizing but without complacency either, the author describes the physical and psychological repercussions of her hero's self-destructive impulse.

Awarded the prestigious Houghton Mifflin Literary Fellowship, Dorothy Baker's novel was published in France in 1948. The translator? Musician and writer Boris Vian, a fan of Bix's and something of a trumpet player himself. Drummer Claude "Doddy" Léon, his faithful companion, had this to say in Noël Arnaud's work *Les Vies parallèles de Boris Vian* (1981):

When it comes to trumpet players who play like Bix, not imitators but people inspired by him, there aren't very many in jazz. Boris Vian had that voluptuous, romantic, very flowery style, nothing like the hard edge of the great trumpet masters of the time.

Whatever the case, *Young Man with a Horn* had such success that Hollywood was eager to bring it to the big screen. The project was entrusted to Michael Curtiz, whose film *Mildred Pierce*, based on the detective novel by James M. Cain, helped earn Joan Crawford an Oscar for best female actress in 1946. The same year, Curtiz directed *Night and Day*, a loose biopic about Cole Porter starring Cary Grant (more about him later). The screen adaptation of Dorothy Baker's book came out in 1950 with Kirk Douglas in the lead, though he was a little too old for the starring role, having beat out other candidates including James Stewart (Curtiz's first choice), Mel Ferrer, and Ronald Reagan. A fresh-faced trumpeter, more interested in his music than in women, the screen version of Rick Martin features a soupçon of ambivalence that could have led the audience to wonder about his sexual orientation. I suppose that was the reason behind the choice of an actor who projected the virile image so dear to American cinema, especially at the time.

Written by Carl Foreman (who contributed the screen-play for *High Noon*, anonymously because of McCarthyism) and Edmund H. North (who with Francis Ford Coppola won the Oscar for best original screenplay for *Patton* in 1970), the film kicks off with a monologue from Willie "Smoke" Willoughby, the hero's confidant, played by Hoagy

Carmichael himself, sitting at his piano and speaking directly into the camera. "My name is Willie Willoughby," he says, "but they call me Smoke. I palled around with Rick Martin, the famous trumpet player. We were in the thankless business of piecing little notes and phrases of music together into a mumbo jumbo that somehow turned out to be jazz."

The movie gives Smoke a promotion by making him the white narrator of the hero's rise and fall. Considering how close he was to Bix, Carmichael must have been a valuable source of counsel for Douglas when it came to playing the young man with the horn. Though it turned Smoke into a Caucasian, the script does not sidestep the racial issues that are fundamental to Baker's novel. For the role of Black trumpeter Art Hazzard, Rick Martin's idol and mentor, the production chose the Puerto Rican actor Juano Hernández instead of Louis Armstrong, who had been slated for the part. His agent Joe Glasner wrote to production manager Steve Trilling that Satchmo would "not only prove himself to be a valuable asset to the picture, but will do justice to any part given to him." Unfortunately for the film, not to take anything away from Hernández, whose performance was adequate but no more, by deciding not to cast Armstrong, the production missed the chance to add an extra touch of authenticity that would have built on Carmichael's presence. In addition, for Hazzard's solos, the team hired a certain Jimmy Zito, "one of the finest trumpet players of the day" according to the promotion notes – a name that to my knowledge is not part of any history of jazz.

It's clear that the desire for authenticity was not among the main motivations of the undertaking. Rick Martin's solos were entrusted to Harry James, the trumpet superstar of the swing era. His sound was grandiloquent, exuberant with vibrato, and had nothing in common with the introverted lyricism associated with Beiderbecke, the distant precursor of cool jazz. That's only the beginning when you consider the complete disconnect between the esthetics of Martin and James as portrayed in the film's cinematographic language. Those esthetics were wholly outdated when compared to the real avant-garde movement – the be-bop style – that had taken over the world of jazz at least five years before *Young Man with a Horn* hit the nation's big screens.

As in *Mildred Pierce*, Michael Curtiz seemed less concerned with realism than with making a dark moral drama (quite successfully done, admittedly) with film noir tones – something he excelled at. In terms of moral universes, I am tempted to see in Amy North – the pseudo-intellectual aristocrat played by Lauren Bacall who marries Rick Martin because she doesn't know what else to do – as the double of the character of Veda, the daughter of the woman who gives her name to the previous film. In Veda, we have a snobbish woman who looks down on her mother who has entered the sub-classes, stooping to work as a waitress in a nightclub. To make matters worse, Veda moves her body lasciviously to the syncopated beat of a jazz band, since she is its lead singer. Hard to fall any lower for a rich heiress who was supposed to have a career as a concert pianist. The character of Amy is a blasé, spoiled doctor's daughter who is pursuing studies in psychiatry, since she can't properly play a Chopin nocturne. She freely admits she envies Rick for his ability to concentrate on a single passion, though she disdains his vulgar music for its African origins.

As much for Veda as it is for Amy, jazz is a form of expression wholly without refinement, and its performers are ordinary public entertainers. The first time Rick and Amy meet at Galba's Club where Rick goes to jam with Art Hazzard's group after his lucrative sets as a lead soloist with Phil Morrison's orchestra (Paul Whiteman's fictitious double), Amy denigrates jazz.

> AMY – I didn't come here to listen to it. I came to study the people, watch their faces. They're interesting. Something about jazz releases inhibitions. It's a sort of cheap, mass-produced narcotic.
> RICK – I gather you don't like jazz.
> AMY – Not particularly. I know it's supposed to be our native art. Cotton fields, the levees, New Orleans and blues in the night.

Rick has a couple good reasons for turning to drink (or at least, he would say so). First, his loveless marriage with Amy, and then the death of Art Hazzard that he could have prevented if he'd listened to the man. Rick already had a tendency to reach for the bottle, but now he's on an all-out campaign. He quits Morrison's orchestra, and spends sleepless nights drinking and playing in a dive with Smoke and other musicians, though the next morning they have a gig in studio to play behind singer Jo Jordan (played by Doris Day) on her new album. Jordan is an old friend of Rick's who would have liked to be more. And then, in the middle of his solo on "With a Song in My Heart," the unthinkable happens. Jo has idolized Rick from the first time they met, but suddenly his high-flying technique deserts him and his improvisation breaks down in the middle of a phrase. The same thing happened to Charlie Parker in 1945, in the middle of a stumbling version of "Lover Man." The session ended with Parker being interned.

Smoke hurriedly interrupts the recording and sends the musicians out of the studio. But it is too late. Rick heard what his colleagues think of him. Humiliated by the general consensus that he's at the end of his rope, he insists on being left alone in the studio and ends up smashing his trumpet in a fit of rage. In the days that follow, to the sound of a particularly syrupy rendition of "Moanin' Low" by Harry James, we watch Rick Martin get ever drunker as he lapses into complete depression, until a cab driver picks him out of the gutter, unconscious, and drives him to a detox clinic. When Smoke hears the news, he runs to the bedside of the fallen jazzman, with Jo in all her beauty showing up soon afterward.

Whereas Dorothy Baker's novel ends with the death of the young man with the horn, felled, like Bix, by a case of pneumonia as a result of his excesses, Hollywood and its audience would not tolerate such a dénouement. Though Jo herself is an artist, she sermonizes to Rick about the impossibility of reaching salvation through music. Then

Michael Curtiz serves up the end of the soliloquy that Smoke began the film with. "Rick was a pretty hard guy to understand," we are told, "and for a long time, he didn't understand himself." But what an artist the man was...

Certainly, the playful tone of the epilogue stands in violent contrast with the lugubrious intro that seemed to predict the worst for Rick Martin. That's Hollywood! Since American commercial movies all need a happy ending, it's no surprise that the last scene features another take of the recording of "With a Song in My Heart" – with Jo radiant and Rick triumphing on his horn.

The End.

∼

Compare this melodrama, an entertainment but no more than that, with *Bix* by the Italian director Pupi Avati, a film that came out in 1991. At first it might seem like an exemplar of historical authenticity. But not so fast. The subtitle gives away what's happening: *Un'ipotesi leggendaria* ("An Interpretation of the Legend"). And we should expect as much, since Avati made two excellent films in the fantastic mode based on the legends of the Po River area, *The House with Laughing Windows* (1976) and *Le Strelle nel Fosso* (1978), and also *Dancing Paradise* (1982), which were less concerned with factual veracity than poetic tribute. All the same, Pupi Avati and his brother Amaro bought and renovated the Beiderbecke house in Davenport to shoot many of the film's scenes.

Stylized and clean, the film begins in October 1931 as Charles Burnette Beiderbecke (played by Mark Collver) arrives in New York, two months after the death of his younger brother (Bryant Weeks). Burnie has come to learn more about his brother's last weeks, and he meets violinist Giuseppe "Joe" Venuti (Emile Levisetti) who was Bix's confrère in Jean Goldkette's orchestra.

I wonder, in a friendly way, of course, whether ethnocentrism pushed Avati to choose Venuti, rather than Trumbauer or Carmichael, to pilot us through Beider-becke's universe. Though as a character, Venuti was no slouch. He was a colorful joker, changing the story of his origins over and over again, which seems to have amused him. His life was a moving target, and the sources claim he was born anywhere between 1894 and 1906. Considered the founding father of jazz violin, just as his childhood friend Eddie Lang (whose real name was Salvatore Massaro) was considered one of the pioneers of jazz guitar, Venuti not only participated in several historic recordings by Beiderbecke and Trumbauer, but he also played on stage and on records with the heavyweights of jazz and jazzy variety until his death in 1978. For example, Bing Crosby, Benny Goodman, the Dorsey Brothers, the Boswell Sisters, and even Zoot Sims, who was his preferred partner in the 1970s.

Venuti tells Burnie about his younger brother's begin-nings, as well as his high and low points, back when he was the star soloist in Paul Whiteman's orchestra (Curtis N. Wollan), America's most famous big band. Together, they go looking for Liza (Sally Groth), the girl whom Bix spoke of in his letters to his family as his betrothed, though he scarcely knew her. Despite hopes for authenticity due to the careful reconstitution of the period, most of the time the film is submerged in fantasies and incongruities and spontaneous invention. That might be justified by the fact that the story of Bix's life was entrusted to a notorious myth-maker who enjoyed maintaining a cloud of artistic uncertainty around his own existence. Though I doubt Pupi had thought of that alibi...

The film is a patchwork of flashbacks narrated by Venuti, though none reaches back any earlier than 1921. There is no reference to the influence of the Original Dixieland Jazz Band on our young man with the cornet. That said, the movie does present the encounters with Paul Mares in Chicago and the impact they had on the future star of the Jazz Age. And we see the friendship between Beiderbecke and the young Hoagy Carmichael (Romano Orzari), and the debut of the Wolverines, and a number of Bix's performances with the Goldkette and Whiteman orchestras along with other white bands he played with. From a musical point of view, the recreation of the sound of the different ensembles is worth lending an ear to. The soundtrack was entrusted to Bob Wilber, a well-known disciple of Benny Goodman, and Wilber turned to cornetist Tom Pletcher, who had been leading a band since 1973. Its name made its intentions clear: The Sons of Bix. Pletcher went on to found the Bix Beiderbecke Memorial Society and a second group, the Bix Centennial Band, very active on the swing circuit, especially on the occasion of the Bix 100th Birthday Cruise.

Even more than Curtiz in *Young Man with a Horn*, Avati seems intent on erasing any trace of the influence of Black musicians and their music on Beiderbecke. By giving a certain stature to the character of Art Hazzard (he was there thanks to Dorothy Baker's novel) in Rick Martin's life, *Young Man* recognizes the debt the latter owed to the former. Of course, the student has to surpass the teacher. In *Bix*, an Italian production, we see the usual parade of background Black domestics and workers who filled the Hollywood films of the times. But there wasn't even a shadow of one of those "real hot jazz musicians" that had Beiderbecke so enthusiastic. Yes, there was that sequence at the Cinderella Ballroom in New York when one of the house musicians proudly remarks that the place is crowded to capacity every night, even if he has to admit afterward that Fletcher Henderson accomplishes the same feat at the Roseland – especially now that he hired the kid who used to play with King Oliver. "Armstrong," says an off-screen voice. The musician nods and adds, "Everybody's going nuts about him. He's pretty tough to beat."

And that's it. End of the discussion.

The film maintains the silence surrounding the most famous jazz artist of the time. Silence will also enshroud his colleagues whose names have become monuments: Fletcher Henderson, Duke Ellington, Coleman Hawkins, Earl Hines – just to name a few. For reasons never explained, Avati does not mention a single one of them, not even in a variation of the scene in many American films where the Black mentor, whether it's Art Hazzard in *Young Man* or Kid Ory in *The Benny Goodman Story* (1956), humbly gives way to the brilliant white student who has naturally outstripped him.

~

Too often, human history is a comedy of errors and omissions. The destiny of Bix Beiderbecke, the archetype of the *jazzman maudit*, lends itself too easily to fantasy and myth-making, and too many people have not bothered with the ordinary facts. The day after his death, if we believe Jean Pierre Lion's biography, Hugues Panassié of the Hot Club de France wrote in October of 1931 that the notice of Beiderbecke's death on August 7 (mistaken on the date) threw the jazz community into despair (excuse the hyperbole). In other words, the music lover who would like to know the truth about the man's life and work would be better off reading biographies like Lion's or watching Brigitte Berman's documentary *Bix: Ain't None of Them Play Like Him Yet* (1981).

One uncertain dawn on a Sunday in June, as I listened to the recording of "In a Mist" that Bix cut by himself, alone at the piano, I thought of the conversation between his cinematic doppelganger, Rick Martin, and the pianist Smoke Willoughby in *Young Man with a Horn*. Rick suggests they make their own music, the way they want to. No way, Smoke retorts, no one will buy records like that. The two of them could disappear tomorrow, Smoke goes on, and no one would be the wiser.

The conclusion is informed by the cynicism typical of Michael Curtiz's films, but it does speak its truth. Sometimes, unfortunately, during their lifetime, talented artists work without anyone really caring about what they are creating and the conditions in which they must carry on. That was as true for Bix Beiderbecke, a star soloist in the top orchestras, as it was for Fats Navarro, Clifford

Brown, Booker Little, or Lee Morgan. Like him, they all passed through. In their areas of endeavor, we could say the same about Vincent van Gogh, Franz Kafka, or any other of the murdered Mozarts. The list is long, so I'll keep it short.

Too often, artists of that quality disappear with hardly a sound, into a fog.

In a mist, you might say.

Black and Blue (I)

On April 4, 1968, Reverend Martin Luther King was gunned down by the enemies of progress.

More than fifty years later, despite certain advancements, the living conditions of the great majority of African Americans have not reached the level of King's utopian vision put forward on the steps of the Lincoln Memorial in Washington, D.C. on August 28, 1963, in his "I Have a Dream" speech that still brings tears to this writer's eyes.

Back in those days, and we can say it's still the same today, there was a world of difference between the dream and its realization. Just two weeks after the march on Washington orchestrated by King and his followers, on September 15, four little Black girls were killed in the bombing of a Baptist church on 16th Street in Birmingham, Alabama. In reaction to the attack for which the Ku Klux Klan took responsibility, saxophonist John Coltrane, one of the most revolutionary and influential artists of modern jazz, composed "Alabama," a requiem for the murdered girls.

On November 18, Coltrane's quartet entered Rudy Van Gelder's studio in Englewood Cliffs, New Jersey, to record this slow, solemn, elegiac piece haunted by the ghosts of those four victims. Coltrane said nothing about it, either to the technicians or his own musicians. That day, the group recorded five takes. One of them, surprisingly enough, ended up on *Live at Birdland* (Impulse!, 1964); the rest of the album was recorded at the famous New York club. Listen to the piece just once and you will understand that Coltrane is using his sax as an instrument of prayer. The poignant melody not only expresses sadness at the deaths of the girls, it traces back the endless chain of injustice that launched the civil rights movement. Filmmaker Spike Lee felt the emotional charge of "Alabama" and used it wisely in his documentary about the bombing, *4 Little Girls* (1997).

On December 7, Coltrane and his group displayed the same sense of meditativeness when they played the piece on *Jazz Casual*, a public television show hosted by critic Ralph J. Gleason. Anyone who's curious can watch that crucial moment on DVD (*John Coltrane: Ralph Gleason's Jazz Casual*, Rhino Home Video, 2003) or on YouTube.

Jack DeJohnette's trio undertook a rereading of the piece on their record *In Movement* (2016), and their version is absolutely worth listening to. For the occasion, the veteran drummer turned to Ravi Coltrane on sax and Matthew Garrison on bass and electronic effects – respectively the sons of John Coltrane and Jimmy Garrison, the bass player in the elder Coltrane's classic quartet.

~

"Alabama" was not the first or the last time a jazz artist lent their talent to the Black cause. By its very origins that reach back to the cotton plantations of the days of slavery in the American South, jazz has always been intimately related to African American history. African slaves and their descendants were stripped of their language, religion, and even their names by their masters, and they were allowed only one means of expression for their despair, one way of finding the courage to work, and that was singing the songs they improvised together under the burning sun of the "gallant South." These work songs would lead the way to Negro spirituals and their profane offspring – the blues, ragtime, and finally jazz.

It may be paradoxical that a music born of the constant oppression, pain, and humiliation of an entire people ended up as one of the premier sources of entertainment in proper American society. But is that really so surprising? From 1929 onward, 12 years after jazz made its debut on phonograph records, pianist and singer Fats Waller, whom some accused of being an ordinary showman, wrote the music for a song by Harry Brooks and Andy Razaf, "(What Did I Do to Be So) Black and Blue?" Staged on Broadway by Edith Wilson, the musical *Connie's Hot Chocolates* featured two other immortal Fats Waller tunes, "Ain't Misbehavin'" and "Honeysuckle Rose." As for "Black and Blue," it went back to the blues tradition, with its notes of sadness mixed with humor used to express the difficulties of Black living conditions in the USA in the 1920s.

Cold empty bed, springs hard as lead
Feel like old Ned, wish I was dead
All my life through, I've been so black and blue

Even the mouse ran from my house
They laugh at you, and scorn you too
What did I do to be so black and blue?

Star trumpet player Louis Armstrong would join the cast of *Connie's Hot Chocolates* some time after it was first staged, and he made the song his own. It soon became one of the crown jewels of his repertoire, and his gravelly voice gave the words the appropriate gravitas. "My only sin is in my skin," he sang on the old 78 cut the year the musical was first performed, refuting those critics who said he wasn't interested in Black issues. Strangely, Fats Waller never recorded this landmark song in his collected works, which was made up of some 20 songs. He ended up selling copyright to publisher Irving Mills for next to nothing, cutting himself out of considerable royalties in the process. Knowing that, we can go back and ask the same question. What did I do to be so black and blue?

Ten years later, it was Billie Holiday's turn to push back against Southern racial prejudice by adding "Strange Fruit" to her repertoire. Considered the first protest song in the history of American popular music, it is based on a poem written and published in 1937 by Abel Meeropol, a teacher of Russian Jewish background who lived in the Bronx and was active in the American Communist Party. Under the pseudonym Lewis Allan, Meeropol set it to music himself with the help of his wife, Black singer Laura Duncan. She was the first to sing it in Madison Square Gardens in 1938. The song is a mighty charge against racism in the United States, and particularly against the lynching of Black Americans that was reaching epidemic proportions in the South.

If we believe the Tuskegee Institute, 3,833 people were lynched between 1889 and 1940. Ninety percent of these summary executions took place in the Southern states, and four victims out of five were Black. In 1939, when Billie added the song to her show at the Café Society, ignoring the advice of John H. Hammond, her producer at Columbia Records, three lynchings had already been perpetrated that year, and a poll revealed that six out of ten whites were in favor of the practice. In Meeropol's words, Billie "gave a startling, most dramatic and effective interpretation, which could jolt an audience out of its complacency anywhere."

The "strange fruit" fought over by crows, turned rotten by the sun, was nothing else but the body of a young Black man hanging from the branches of a tree. Meeropol's second verse leaves no doubt, with its evocation of "bulging eyes" and "twisted mouth" mixed in with the perfume of magnolias.

No wonder John Hammond, though a progressive, categorically refused to let Billie record the song on Columbia. The label still intended to do business in the Southern states. And "Strange Fruit" did stand out in Lady Day's repertory. Up until then it consisted of standards, Broadway show tunes, and a large number of lamentations of women unhappy in love, cheated on, mistreated, even beaten by heartless brutes with no self-respect. Billie had to get a derogation of her contract to record her emblematic song with a small independent label, Commodore, founded by Milt Gabler. Billie was well known in the US, but the recording of "Strange Fruit" brought her international acclaim, and it climbed to the 16th spot on the charts in July 1939. Her public image became so closely associated with the song that, several years later, she wanted to use the final words, "bitter crop" as the title of her autobiography. This, her publisher refused.

Not surprisingly, the FBI considered Lady Day an artist in revolt, a subversive, even a Communist. The authorities harassed her ceaselessly, charging her with drug offenses, confiscating her cabaret card without which an entertainer cannot perform in the New York nightclubs. Until the end of her brief life, Billie sang "Strange Fruit" at the end of every show, like a ritual. On the first two studio takes (*The Complete Commodore Recordings, 1939 – 1944,* GRP 1987), she delivers an intensity and emotional quality that no singer, not even her in her later versions, has ever equaled or surpassed.

Still, we shouldn't deny the value of later interpretations by other artists. There is Nina Simone's very theatrical version on *Pastel Blues* (Philips, 1956), and Simone was certainly a leading voice in the civil rights movement. Jeanie Bryson delivers a take more recited than sung on trumpeter Terence Blanchard's *The Billie Holiday Songbook* (Columbia, 1994). Cassandra Wilson came up with two versions on *Blue Light 'Til Dawn* (Blue Note, 1993) and *Coming Forth by Day* (Legacy, 2015), an homage to Billie for her centenary. José James, a jazz soul crooner, used gospel accents in his very affecting *a capella* take on *Yesterday I Had the Blues: The Music of Billie Holiday* (Blue Note, 2015), also commemorating her centenary. Closer to our time, the Haitian-Montreal singer Dominique Fils-Aimé made the song her own, with aplomb and audacity on her first record *Nameless* (Ensoul, 2018), inspired by the spirit of the African American poet Maya Angelou.

The Black British diva Rebecca Ferguson's homage to Billie (*Lady Sings the Blues*, RCA, 2015) certainly doesn't set the world on fire. Still, I would have liked to hear this artist – she was discovered through the televised music competition *X Factor* – sing the hymn against lynching at Donald Trump's inauguration in January 2017, as she ironically offered to do. But no one ever acknowledged her proposal.

~

On July 12, 2018, the *New York Times* informed us that the federal government had discreetly reopened its inquiry into the murder of Emmett Till, an astonishing development in the Trump era. Some sixty years after the event, the murder of the 14-year-old young Black man is among the most gruesome examples of racial violence in the gallant South – and was one of the major impetuses for the civil rights movement.

In August 1955, Emmett was sent to his great-uncle Moses Wright in Money, Mississippi. The boy had received strict instructions from his mother to mind his manners with white people. In Mississippi, more than 500 African Americans had been lynched since 1882, and racially motivated murder was a common occurrence, especially in the Delta. Racial tensions had been exacerbated on May 17,

1954, by the NAACP's historical victory at the US Supreme Court, which recognized that segregated schools went against the Constitution (the *Brown v. Board of Education* judgment).

On August 24, Emmett and some other Black teens, workers' sons who had picked cotton all day, went to Bryant's grocery store to buy some cold drinks. The place belonged to Roy and Carolyn Bryant, a white couple, and only the woman was there that day. According to Simeon Wright, Emmett's cousin, the daring boy whistled at Mrs. Bryant on the way out of the store. He wanted to show the other guys that, since he came from up North, he could do things that were otherwise not allowed in the South.

Carolyn Bryant would put forward several other versions. Emmett whistled at her. He spoke to her in a vulgar manner. She even maintained that Till put his arm around her waist and offered a tryst with these words: "You needn't be afraid of me, baby. I've been with white women before." Terrorized, Carolyn ran to her car for her pistol to chase away the boys. Before her husband came back from his business trip, all Tallahatchie County knew what had happened. The gossips learned about the incident and whispered that Emmett and Carolyn were having an affair.

On the night of August 28, around 2:30 in the morning, Roy Bryant and his half-brother J. W. Milam kidnapped Emmett Till at gunpoint from his great-uncle's house. They took him to a shed on a plantation in the next county and beat him until he was unrecognizable. They tore out his eyes and threw him into the Tallahatchie River alive. When they were questioned about the boy's disappearance, Bryant and

Milam swore to Sheriff Clarence Strider, who played the role of Pontius Pilate, that when they discovered Till wasn't the one who had insulted Mrs. Bryant, they let him go.

An unprecedented investigation led by local police and journalists and even the NAACP led to a trial that began on September 19. Four days later, a jury of 12 white men acquitted the two accused after just 72 minutes of deliberation. The next year, in the pages of the magazine *Look*, the two men freely confessed to their guilt, counting on their impunity, since according to the Double Jeopardy Clause of the Fifth Amendment, no person shall be judged twice for the same offense. According to their version of the story, they didn't want to kill the boy, just impress him, but since he kept provoking them, they increased the punishment.

In 1956, the poets began weighing in. First, from Senegal, David Diop dedicated a poem to Till's memory in his collection *Coups de Pilon* (Présence africaine), and he was soon followed by Aimé Césaire from Martinique in *Ferrements* (Seuil, 1960). Bob Dylan was the first to write a song about the event that caused an uproar in the US and Europe ("The Death of Emmett Till," 1962). Strangely, several decades went by before jazz artists turned their talents to this horrible story. There was guitarist Russell Malone ("Flowers for Emmett Till," 1992), sax player Ernest Dawkins ("Un-Till Emmett Till," 2008), and most recently, avant-garde trumpeter Wadada Leo Smith ("Emmett Till: Defiant, Fearless," on his monumental *Ten Freedom Summers*, Cuneiform, 2012). On the vocal scene, Melody Gardot established a connection between Till and Trayvon

Martin, Michael Brown, and Eric Garner, all contemporary victims of American systemic racism ("Preacherman" on *Currency of Man*, Decca, 2015).

∿

After the murder of Emmett Till, the Rosa Parks story was quick to inspire creative minds. A key figure in the struggle against racial segregation in the US, she entered the annals of history on December 1, 1955, in Montgomery, Alabama when she refused to give up her spot to a white passenger in a city bus. The police arrested her, and she was fined 15 dollars. Very quickly, on December 5, she appealed the judgment. A young Black pastor, only 26 years old, by the name of Martin Luther King organized a boycott of the Montgomery bus system. That campaign lasted over a year and set the civil rights movement on its way.

"She sat down in order that we all might stand up," Jesse Jackson would say at the great lady's funeral in 2005. "Paradoxically, her imprisonment opened the doors for our long journey to freedom." Musicians were quick to follow. In 1957, trumpet player Clark Terry paid tribute to Rosa Parks' action with his "Serenade to a Bus Seat." The piece lent its name to his album on Riverside.

On the soul music shelf, the New Orleans group the Neville Brothers sang "Sister Rosa" (*Yellow Moon*, A&M, 1989), and the French singer Ben l'Oncle Soul praised Parks' convictions in "Soul Man" (*Ben l'Oncle Soul*, Motown France, 2010). On her album *Touch* (Origin, 2010), pianist and composer Jessica Williams dedicated her piece "Rosa

Parks" to the civil rights icon. On January 25 and 26, 2013, at Lincoln Theater, the Columbus Jazz Orchestra under the direction of Byron Stripling proudly celebrated the courage, dignity, and legacy of "the mother of the modern Civil Rights Movement" with "Suite Rosa," composed by John Clayton to mark the centenary of her birth and commemorate that historic day in December 1955. In Toulouse, France in 2014, singer Diane Launay and guitarist Clément Grondin formed the Rosa Parks duo to express their passion for the songs of Billie Holiday and Nina Simone.

And on February 4, 2019, Ms. Parks' birthday, trumpeter Wadada Leo Smith issued an oratorio of seven arias entitled *Rosa Parks: Pure Love* (TUM Records).

∿

But let's go back to May 17, 1954, and the decision to put an end to school segregation, which was confirmed in 1955 by an Eisenhower administration decree. Indignant, the Southern states used local laws to restrict Black teenagers from attending white schools. Claiming he wanted to avoid a riot, the governor of Arkansas, Orval Eugene Faubus, a Democrat, called out the National Guard to keep nine Black students from entering Little Rock Central High School. To protect the "Little Rock Nine," the federal government sent in soldiers from the 101st Airborne Division. On September 12, 1958, Faubus ordered all schools to be closed rather than accept integrated classrooms. The next year, bassist Charles Mingus wrote and composed a scorching reply to the governor, his famous "Fables of Faubus." Though the piece may be better known as an instrumental, Mingus did write shouted lyrics for it, rhyming "ridiculous" with "supremacist."

History, we know by now, has an unfortunate way of repeating itself. Columbia Records, which refused to record "Strange Fruit" 20 years earlier so as not to anger potential Southern customers, would not let Mingus include the sung version of "Fables" on his album *Mingus Ah Um* (1960), allowing only the instrumental version. His fans would have to wait until 1961 to hear the bassist's song under a new title, "Original Faubus Fables," on the LP *Charles Mingus Presents Charles Mingus* on Candid Records, an independent, free-thinking label.

In his 1962 article for the *American Record Guide*, critic Don Heckman described that cut as "a classic Negro put-down in which satire becomes a deadly rapier-thrust. Faubus emerges in the glare of ridicule as a mock villain whom no-one really takes seriously. This kind of commentary, brimful of feeling, bitingly direct and harshly satiric, appears far too rarely in jazz."

Among musicians who have revisited "Fables of Faubus," we find sax player Gerry Mulligan, vibraphonist Lionel Hampton, guitarist Charlie Hunter, and the Jacob Fred Jazz Odyssey. The Mingus Big Band, a group dedicated to advancing the work of the late bassist, paid tribute to the song on *Gunslinging Birds* (Dreyfus, 1995), with pianist Kenny Drew Jr. adding references associated with Southern traditions (in "I Wish I Was in Dixie," among others) to underscore Mingus' contempt for racism. The piece can also be heard on *Mingus Erectus* (Ambiances magnétiques,

2005) by bassist Normand Guilbeault, a Montreal Mingus disciple, in a version renamed for his historical moment: "Fable of (George Dubya) Faubus," with lyrics that go after George W. Bush.

~

Throughout the 1960s, the civil rights movement would intensify on a number of fronts, and several essential figures would step forward, including Medgar Evers, Malcom X, and Martin Luther King – all assassinated in cowardly fashion in 1963, 1965, and 1968, respectively. The Black Panthers had their day, and violence exploded in the country's ghettos. Many jazz artists would echo the profound social upheaval that resulted from the demands of the Black population.

Lady Sings the Blues

How painful it is to revisit old loves that have lost the charm we once found in them! I had that thought as I watched the biopic *Lady Sings the Blues* (1972), directed by Sidney J. Furie, with Diana Ross in the role of Billie Holiday.

I was 13 years old when I first saw the film on TV. I was watching it with my mother, whom we called Lady I., and I had no idea who the singer was – the one being portrayed by the princess of Motown, that is. I knew only that I had a teenage passion for Diana Ross. In my humble opinion, she was the best singer and the most beautiful woman in the world.

Please forgive my teenage infatuation!

Loosely adapted from the biography of the diva, a simple compilation of old interviews collected by journalist William Dufty, *Lady Sings the Blues* opens with the singer getting arrested in New York for the possession and use of narcotics. The year is 1945. A flashback takes us to 1928, when the young Eleanora Fagan (her birth name) is working as a cleaner in a whorehouse in Baltimore, where she is sexually assaulted.

After a stint in a correctional facility, Eleanora settles in Harlem with her mother, herself a chambermaid in a house of ill repute. The arrogant owner hires the girl, though he underpays her. Tired of scrubbing the floors, the future jazz vocal star turns to prostitution. Piano Man, the whorehouse piano player (played by comedian Richard Pryor) encourages her to audition in a nightclub for a job as a dancer, but she fails the test. Yet when Jerry, the club owner, hears her rendition of "All of Me" with Piano Man backing her up, he decides to take her on as a singer. Using the stage name Billie Holiday, her success is modest at best. But one night, Louis McKay (Billie's three husbands rolled into one and played by the suave Billy Dee Williams) leaves her a generous tip. She hesitates too long for Jerry's taste, but then picks up the banknote, slips it into her bra, and bursts into "Them There Eyes."

From the very first songs Diana Ross sang in her role as Billie Holiday, there in our living room, my mother frowned. Coproduced by Motown, the film seemingly sets out to tell the tragic story of Billie Holiday, but its real mission is to advance the career of Ross, the ex-leader of The Supremes, who was also the record boss' mistress. Without exactly imitating Lady Day, Diana Ross adopts some of the mannerisms typical of the diva she is supposed to represent.

"What she does with the songs is all right, but nothing of Billie Holiday's caliber," my mother declared.

I nearly blew a gasket! I considered Diana Ross above all criticism, and badmouthing her was a crime of lèse-majesté. "Don't take my word for it, Stan," my mother added. "If you're interested, we have the real Billie's records right over there. Feel free to look through my collection, listen, and decide for yourself." I didn't fall in love immediately, but time would do its work and the presumptuous teenager would soon learn the difference between Diana Ross and Billie Holiday.

Hollywood had toyed with the idea of a big-screen version of Billie's memoirs from the time they were published in 1956. Anthony Mann hoped to direct the adaptation with Dorothy Dandridge as the star, and she was also the favorite for several other productions, and even for a musical that never got off the ground. In the 1960s, actor-director-screenwriter Ossie Davis publicly declared his intention of filming the story with Abbey Lincoln in the role of the woman who had such influence on him. Then, having acquired the rights to Billie's book, in 1969 producer Jay Weston signed a deal with Cinema Center Films for the production of a biopic. Diahann Carroll, Lola Falana, and Cicely Tyson were all candidates to play incarnate Billie, until Berry Gordy, Motown's big boss, got involved in the production and imposed his choice. It would be Diana Ross, a controversial move. At the time, Ross' experience as an actress could be summed up by a number of humorous sketches on TV and an appearance in an episode of the series *Tarzan* with Ron Ely, in which her sisters from The Supremes played nuns on a mission to Africa.

For years, Ross maintained that she had always been an all-out fan of Billie Holiday and loved it when people who had enjoyed the movie actually thought she was Billie when they saw her on the street. The truth was different. She discovered the music at the time she recorded the songs orchestrated for her by trumpeter and arranger Gil

Askey. According to Tom Milne of the British publication *The Monthly Film Bulletin*, Diana Ross did "a remarkable pastiche job on the tone and timbre of Billie Holiday's voice, [but] misses the elegant, almost literary wit of her phrasing." But what did that matter? The soundtrack album soon became the fourth of Diana Ross' records to sit atop the charts (though the first solo effort), with sales of more than two million copies in the United States alone, which made it one of Motown's bestsellers.

In 1992, to celebrate the 20th anniversary of her homage to Billie and revive her back-burner career, Diana Ross returned to the modest jazz section of her discography with *Stolen Moments: The Lady Sings... Jazz and Blues* (Motown, 1993). It was recorded in front of a live audience at New York's Ritz Theater with the support of an orchestra directed by Gil Askey featuring some big-name talent, including trumpeters Jon Faddis and Roy Hargrove and bassist Ron Carter.

As for the film itself, critic Gene Siskel (at the time, writing for *The Chicago Tribune*) gave it three stars out of four, while pointing out that:

> the fact that *Lady Sings the Blues* is a failure as a biography of legendary jazz singer Billie Holiday doesn't mean it can't be an entertaining movie. And it is just that – entertaining – because of an old fashioned *grand dame* performance by Diana Ross, late of the pop-rock scene, in the title role.

Normally operating in a harsher tone, Pauline Kael of *The New Yorker* weighed in as follows:

When the movie was over I wrote "I love it" on my pad of paper... Factually it's a fraud, but emotionally it delivers. It has what makes movies work for a mass audience: easy pleasure, tawdry electricity, personality – great quantities of personality.

In other words, the doubts people might have had about Ross' ability to take on this demanding role disappeared when *Lady Sings the Blues* had its theatrical release. Even the detractors of the screenplay, who said it was full of clichés and historically inaccurate, were charmed by her sincere performance which earned her a Golden Globe and an Oscar nomination. The real problem with the film does not lie in its star's interpretation or her shortcomings as a singer. The movie is based on the original artist's memoir, and in its pages she was more concerned with polishing her monument to herself, and magnifying her own legendary status, than telling what really happened. The three screenwriters (Chris Clark, Terence McCloy, and Suzanne De Passe) could hardly be expected to avoid half-truths, unreal sequences, and incongruous moments.

We know, for example, that Billie was born in Philadelphia and not Baltimore, but the rest of her childhood is cloaked in obscurity. In his biography *Billie Holiday* (Northeastern University Press, 1995), the British writer Stuart Nicholson states that her birth certificate identifies her father as a certain Frank DeViese, whereas the singer spent her life claiming that she was the daughter of Clarence Holiday, the love of her mother's youth who played guitar in Fletcher Henderson's orchestra.

As a result, we have to pick and choose which facts to believe with this movie. Admittedly, it does depict the rampant racism of the 1930s and tries to link the violence of these experiences to Billie's drug problem. During a tour through the Deep South with an imaginary group of white musicians, Billie, as played by Diana Ross, briefly steps away from the band bus for a breath of fresh air, only to come upon the sight of a Black man hanging from a tree, the victim of a lynching. Later in the movie, the bus is attacked during a Ku Klux Klan parade. These events are fictional, though the real Billie Holiday was often made to use the back door instead of the main entrance the way her white band did. And she was often the object of catcalls and insults from racist audiences.

Though not inaccurate, the episode of the KKK's attack on the bus is echoed by a similar sequence in a recent TV film, *Bessie* (2015). This is director Dee Rees' work on the life and career of one of Billie's idols, Bessie Smith. Crowned "The Empress of the Blues" in the 1920s to the detriment of her spiritual godmother Ma Rainey, Smith, played in excellent fashion by Queen Latifah, crisscrosses the United States on board her private train, sparing her the usual problems of lodging her band in the segregated cities of the South.

Despite that effort, a group of white supremacists attempts to sabotage Bessie's show by attacking the guy wires of the tent that they then intend to set on fire. The imposing singer doesn't think twice. She rushes out of the enormous tent and counterattacks the masked men with her flying fists, before climbing back on stage to continue the show. I always doubted that the scene could have taken place, and figured it was designed to let the audience know just how intrepid a woman Bessie Smith was. But then I discovered that her biography written by Chris Albertson corroborates the reality of the incident that took place in July 1927, even if nothing proves that, as in the film, she threatened her assailants with an axe.

Since *Lady Sings the Blues* became a cinematic standard, most movie portraits of the great African American singers contain one or more similar events, true or made up, showing our heroines facing down racial discrimination in its many more or less virulent forms.

In Brian Gibson's *The Josephine Baker Story* (1991), with Lynn Whitfield in the title role, the former star of "La Revue nègre" briefly returns to her home country. There, at the Stork Club, she will wait over an hour for a steak that will never be served. The non-service is a reprisal for her public position in favor of the civil rights movement.

In *Introducing Dorothy Dandridge* (1999) by Martha Coolidge, the first Black woman artist to receive an Oscar nomination (played by Halle Berry, the first African American to win the golden statuette in 2002) will learn the cost of daring to dip her little toe in the pool at the Last Frontier hotel where she was staying and performing in 1953. To avoid ruffling the feathers of its rich white clientele, the management drained the water out of the pool.

And then there was *Nina* by Cynthia Mort (2016). It is the only filmed biography to have triggered as much controversy before it even hit the screens as *Lady Sings the*

Blues did. The issue was the choice of the actress to portray Nina Simone, the Haitian-Dominican Zoe Saldana, first judged to be too pale of skin color and not Black enough to play the singer. Not to mention certain elements of the screenplay, such as the invented love affair between Nina Simone and her personal nurse who would become her manager, Clifton Henderson, who was gay in real life. This reductive portrait of Simone as a pitiful alcoholic and junkie, erasing her past as a civil rights militant, exudes such racism that we can easily see why Liz Garbus' TV documentary *What Happened, Miss Simone?* (2015), which came out about the same time, had no trouble blowing *Nina* off the screen.

~

Lady Sings the Blues suggests that Billie Holiday's confrontation with Deep South racism gave her the impetus to create "Strange Fruit." A compelling theory, though not particularly more appropriate. Her adoption of the song is a much more complex story. After a tour through the South with clarinetist Artie Shaw's band, Billie took up residence at the chic Café Society in Greenwich Village. Her performances had all New York talking, and everybody's favorites were the torch songs, those sentimental ballads with jilted women telling of their trials, numbers like "I Cover the Waterfront," "My Man," and others along the lines of "Can't Help Lovin' Dat Man."

One evening, a local public school teacher named Abel Meeropol came calling on Barney Josephson, Café Society's owner, to ask him whether Billie would agree to sing a song he co-wrote with his wife, Laura Duncan, who was the first to do a version of it. The song was the controversial "Strange Fruit." Contrary to the story Billie herself told, she did not fall in love with it the moment she heard it. Quite the opposite. In his *33 Revolutions per Minute: A History of Protest Songs, From Billie Holiday to Green Day*, Dorian Lynskey reports that she agreed to take it on only out of regard for Josephson. In Meeropol's words, cited by Lynskey, "To be perfectly frank, I don't think she felt comfortable with the song."

And who could blame her?

It was not the first protest song *per se*, but it was certainly the first in the entertainment field to carry such an explicitly political message. Unlike songs from the trade union movement, "Strange Fruit" is not out to whip up passions, but make the blood run cold. "That is about the ugliest song I have ever heard," Nina Simone would later say, though her version of it is among the most moving. "Ugly in the sense that it is violent and tears at the guts of what white people have done to my people in this country."

"Strange Fruit" was something completely unexpected. Before it, protest songs belonged in the toolbox of left-wing propaganda. But this one proved they could be art.

Try and imagine the shock for the audience filling Café Society, one of the rare racially integrated New York clubs. These people had come to hear the singer in residence, a Black 23-year-old who made a name for herself in Harlem with Count Basie's orchestra. She had golden skin like a Polynesian woman, a full figure, and a white gardenia in her hair.

Throughout the evening's performance, she had the crowd eating out of her hand. Even the lightest ditties took on a depth their writers never knew was there.

Then, suddenly, it happened, out of the blue. The lights went down except for a single harsh spotlight illuminating the singer. It would be her last song of the night.

"Southern trees bear a strange fruit." This was certainly not part of her usual repertory. "Blood on the leaves and blood at the root." What was she talking about? "Black bodies swinging in the Southern breeze." The chitchat at the tables falls silent. Every eye is on the singer, every ear strains to hear. After the last verse that ends with this cry – "Here is a strange and bitter crop" – the spotlight dies, and the club is thrown into darkness. When the lights come back up, Billie is nowhere to be seen.

Imagine the audience trying to figure out how to react... In her book, Billie Holiday remembers the first time she sang the song in front of the startled crowd at Café Society:

> There wasn't even a patter of applause when I finished. Then a lone person began to clap nervously. Then suddenly everyone was clapping.

No number from the Great American Songbook had ever taken on such a subject, so difficult and so sensitive, unacceptable for so-called modern, civilized American society. The only exception might be Irving Berlin's "Supper Time," but the themes in that piece are hinted at more than stated. In this song from the musical *As Thousands Cheer*

(1933), an African American mother thinks twice about setting the table for the evening meal and wonders how to explain their father's absence to her children, for the man will not return. Lynching is not explicitly mentioned in the words, but it is suggested by the context.

Once she saw how powerful a song "Strange Fruit" was, Billie Holiday campaigned to record it, against the advice of her producer at Columbia Records, John Hammond, who was afraid of alienating audiences in the Southern states. A derogation to her contract allowed her to record some 15 songs for Commodore, including "Strange Fruit" on April 20, 1939. The specialized label would issue it in a limited edition. In 1940, a year after the 78 came out, lynching opponents led by the NAACP convinced the House of Representatives to adopt a new bill outlawing the practice. But like those that came before it, it died on the Senate floor.

By then, Billie had stopped singing at Café Society. But wherever she went over the next two decades of her life, she took the song with her, though she sang it less often, and not for just any audience. "She didn't like to sing it because it hurt her so much," said Lee Young, quoted by David Margolick in his *Strange Fruit: Billie Holiday, Café Society, and an Early Cry for Civil Rights* (Running Press, 2000). "She would cry every time she would do it."

She recorded three official versions after the original one from 1939. The last dates from a concert performance in London, taped by the BBC in February 1959. This was a little more than two years after her sold-out triumph at Carnegie Hall which featured the launch of her book *Lady*

Sings the Blues. The concert concludes the film of the same name inspired by her book.

Five months later, she left this vale of tears.

~

In *With Fondest Regards*, French writer Françoise Sagan did a much better job describing Billie's dramatic presence: "She was a femme fatale, in the way fate fell upon her from the very start and never let up." Like all artists of her stature, she is not really gone and will never die. Our collective memory and the recordings that will live forever have granted her a kind of immortality. We can see and hear her again in all her pain and splendor in *Symphony in Black* (1935), a short nine-minute film with Duke Ellington and his orchestra. Subtitled "A Rhapsody of Negro Life," Fred Waller's work is a major landmark in the history of entertainment, culture, and music and a key moment in Duke's and Billie's career.

And there she is again with the same emotion as she returns to a favorite blues, "Fine and Mellow," the B side of the 78 of "Strange Fruit." She was appearing on *The Sound of Jazz* on CBS television, December 8, 1957. Backing her up was a hall of fame of musicians with whom she had played during the swing years: sax men Coleman Hawkins and Ben Webster, trumpet players Doc Cheatham and Roy Eldridge, and pianist Mel Waldron. Off screen, we can hear Billie prefacing the piece:

> The blues to me is like being very sad, very sick, going to church, being very happy. There's two kinds of blues,

happy blues and then sad blues. I don't know, blues is sort of a mixed-up thing. You just have to feel it. Everything I sing is part of my life.

For the occasion, Billie was reunited, and for the last time, with her longtime friend, sax player Lester Young. She called him Prez and he returned the favor by giving her the name Lady Day. The two artists had lost track of one another over the years. Critic Nat Hentoff was part of the production team for *The Sound of Jazz*, and he told how, during the rehearsals, Prez and Lady Day stood at opposite ends of the room. He was sick by then, and weak. During "Fine and Mellow," Ben Webster played the first solo. Then, as Hentoff reported, Lester got up, and he played the purest blues, and it was as if they were both remembering what had been – whatever that was. In the control room everyone was crying. When the show was over, they went their separate ways.

Forever separated. Both would pass less than two years after their last musical reunion.

But immortal all the same…

On April 16, 1986, at Atlanta's Alliance Theater, the curtain went up on *Lady Day at Emerson's Bar and Grill*, a one-woman show for an actress and singer, written by Lanie Robertson. Through a series of dramatic soliloquies and songs, the play tells the story of Billie Holiday's life. Set in a dive in Philadelphia in 1959, the year she died, the play has Billie completely stoned, attempting to make it through her repertory. Robertson gave her larger-than-life lines and a series of heartbreaking monologues that frame her famous songs, which bring us to our knees.

A mainstay of Broadway and elsewhere since it was first created, *Lady Day at Emerson's* also enjoyed a Montreal production starring Ranee Lee, a jazz singer well known in her own right. It was first presented as part of the Montreal International Jazz Festival in 1987, and it spawned an album consecrated to Billie's world, *Deep Song* (Justin Time, 1989). But the show's run in Canada was just beginning. It played at the Centaur Theatre in Montreal and the National Arts Centre in Ottawa, then had top billing in Toronto for nine months, earning Ranee Lee the Dora Mavor Moore Award in 1988. The CTV network went on to broadcast the show in 1994.

More recently, for the production presented at the Circle in the Square Theatre on Broadway in 2014, star actress Audra McDonald received the sixth Tony of her career. The TV show filmed at New Orleans' Cafe Brasil and aired on the HBO network earned her an Emmy nomination in the category of Outstanding Lead Actress in a Limited Series or Movie.

On the other side of the pond, singer, actress, and writer Viktor Lazlo published *My Name Is Billie Holiday* in 2012 (Albin Michel, Paris). The book is a hybrid: part novel, part biography, part autobiography. In January 2013 in Paris, she opened a show adapted from the book at the Théâtre Rive Gauche, directed by Éric-Emmanuel Schmitt. The reception was generally positive, and critics praised Lazlo for not trying to imitate, recreate, or mime Billie Holiday, but simply singing the 20 or so songs she had chosen, with her own voice and manner. Lazlo obviously understood that Lady Day's ways can't be reproduced and that choosing to pastiche her would lead to artistic disaster.

And what is it about Billie Holiday's style that gives her a unique position among jazz singers – or all singers, for that matter? Danièle Robert, the French translator of her book and the author of *Chants de l'aube de Lady Day* (Le temps qu'il fait, 1993), a moving biography of the singer, gives us an idea. It was her pauses, in the folds of the melody, and the question she seems to ask: *What's the point?* Or, more troubling, *Why not?* Weariness, perhaps, a voluptuous letting go. As if, as she is singing, she is listening to an inner mysterious voice.

TragicLee

A Drama in Two Acts

I could find no independent source to corroborate this anecdote, though it has become a jazz legend. Lee Morgan liked telling this story so much that he might just have invented it himself. In the spring of 1963, he was trying to establish himself again in New York after spending some time away from the stage, moving back and forth from his hometown of Philadelphia to the Mecca of jazz. Morgan was a fiery trumpeter who had played in Dizzy Gillespie's big band and with Art Blakey's Jazz Messengers. One evening, he heard the popular DJ Symphony Sid Torin play a special show in his memory on radio station WEVD. I don't know if Morgan, who was 24 at the time when his posthumous tribute ran, was an avid reader of Mark Twain. If he had been, he could have replied with the author's famous claim: "The reports of my death are greatly exaggerated."

That being said, to let Symphony Sid off the hook, and everyone else who repeated the funereal rumor, Lee Morgan, the young wolf of the hard bop school, would never reach the age of 30. Like many musicians of his generation – and despite the tragic outcomes of men like Charlie Parker, Freddie Webster, Fats Navarro, and other junkies who could have dissuaded him from that path – Lee Morgan listened hard to the siren song of drugs. In July 1961, his addiction was so extreme that, like pianist Bobby Timmons before him, he was kicked out of the Jazz Messengers by drummer Art Blakey who, ironically, introduced him to heroin in the first place. That attitude wasn't rare among jazzmen of the time. Charlie Parker always tried to discourage others who wanted to imitate him, thinking they would be able to play the way he did. Parker even had the nerve to claim that he shot up heroin to show people what not to do and what would happen if they got addicted. As mentioned in Bob Reisner's *Bird: The Legend of Charlie Parker* (1977), Blakey added an ambiguous epilogue about the sax player's fate. He claimed that Bird died trying to kick his habit and that he went about it the wrong way, by drinking whiskey; the whiskey was the thing that killed him. A little bit more to the point, Blakey added that our society has to face the fact that people who are using dope are not crazy or criminal: they are sick. The man had been sick for fourteen years and nobody would help him because they didn't know.

Lee Morgan knew very well what heroin was, and he never truly freed himself from its grasp. He also understood the unpleasant consequences of using it. Dealers attacked him in a New York alley and knocked out several of his teeth to teach him a lesson about being late on his payments. The same thing would happen to Chet Baker several years later. Playwright Samuel B. Harps III would take Morgan's up-

and-down career and tumultuous life and turn it all into a play in the 1980s, *Don't Explain*.

But let's not get ahead of ourselves…

The prologue is done. Now the curtain goes up on Act I.

~

The youngest of four children of Otto Ricardo and Nettie Beatrice Morgan, Edward Lee came into this world on July 10, 1938, in Philadelphia. "To tell the truth, I didn't grow up in a family of musicians," Mogie (the nickname his closest friends called him) told François Postif in an interview in *Jazz Magazine* in 1959. "But my oldest sister was an excellent church organist and my father played trombone – I can still remember his sound." At first the vibraphone caught his ear. But at 13 he took up the trumpet after his mother and his sister Ernestine got together to buy him one. He took private lessons, then entered Mastbaum Vocational Technical High School, where he learned to play alto sax. He had been jazz-crazy since he was a kid, and he followed the vibrant local scene, where a fan could see stars like Roy Eldridge, Ella Fitzgerald, Erroll Gardner, Bud Powell, and others. At the time, saxophone players like Benny Golson and John Coltrane were emerging in Philadelphia, along with pianist McCoy Tyner, three musicians Morgan would soon join on stage and on records. The members of the Heath clan were around, too: saxophonist Jimmy, bassist Percy, and drummer Albert – known as "Tootie" – who would all become essential figures in modern jazz.

At the age 15, Lee Morgan started his first combo with bassist James "Spanky" DeBrest. From April of 1954, Morgan took part in the improv workshops held on Tuesday evenings in a community center in north Philadelphia. There, he met giants like Dizzy Gillespie, Miles Davis, and others. If we take Jeffrey S. McMillan's word for it, a trumpet player himself and the author of *Delightful Lee: The Life and Music of Lee Morgan*, Mogie was at the first session that featured a quartet under the direction of trumpeter and singer Chet Baker, the big name in California cool jazz, with James Moody on sax.

According to Mogie's colleague Wilmer Wise, quoted by McMillan, "Chet Baker played there one day, and Lee came up and played – you know, skinny, scrawny, little Lee – and blew Chet Baker completely out of the room. Lee was that kind of player when he was a kid."

In that setting, Morgan met another trumpet prodigy, Clifford Brown, eight years his senior. McMillan's book tells how Brown took him under his wing and made a big impact on his development. Miles Davis was no doubt the first to influence all young trumpet players. He had a relaxed style, which was easy to replicate. But when Morgan first heard Brown playing with a very good rhythm and blues band, he decided that that was how he should play.

The stars were perfectly aligned. The young man from Philadelphia wanted to improve his musical knowledge, and Brownie – as Clifford Brown was called – was happy to share what he knew with the younger man. Morgan had plenty of ambition. Already, he imagined his name on the list of virtuoso trumpet players of the modern era founded by

Diz – Dizzy Gillespie, the heir to Louis Armstrong and Roy Eldridge – and carried on for the next ten years by the late Fats Navarro, who was only passing through, and Brownie. And Morgan had more than ambition. He had talent.

After getting his diploma from Mastbaum, Morgan crossed paths for the first time with drummer Art Blakey, whose famous Jazz Messengers were supposed to play a gig in Philadelphia. But Blakey had a problem. Two members of his group, the trumpeter and the bassist, had gone missing. That was the perfect opportunity. Lee Morgan and Spanky DeBrest were recruited as last-minute substitutes. "Spanky stayed on [with the Messengers]; I could have stayed too, but I didn't want to sign a contract, so I left after two weeks," Morgan explained in the liner notes of *Lee Morgan Indeed!* (Blue Note, 1957), his first album as a leader. "Then very soon after that, Dizzy came back from his South American tour. I'd met him a couple of years before at the workshop and he knew about me. He needed a replacement for Joe Gordon, and I needed some big band experience, so it worked out fine."

Meanwhile, late in the evening of June 25, 1956, Clifford Brown and his pianist Richie Powell got on the road in Powell's brand-new automobile. Their destination was Chicago; they had a date at the Blue Note club the next day. Powell's wife took the wheel so the two musicians would be able to get some sleep. Around one o'clock in the morning, a hard rain started falling on the Pennsylvania Turnpike. The road was slippery, and Nancy Powell lost control of the vehicle. It skidded, crashed, and flipped over several times. All three of them were killed instantly.

It was an absurd way to go for Brownie, the young be-bop prodigy, as absurd as Albert Camus' death in a similar accident four years later. Brown was a musician of exemplary conduct, a good father, a faithful husband – something of an oddity in his line of work. He didn't touch drugs and was not much for drinking. When a gig was over, the young man, affable and calm, would leave the club instead of hanging out. On days when he was recording, he showed up in studio an hour early to take the time to clean his instrument and prepare. In other words, the antithesis of a Charlie Parker. Inconsolable, his friend Sonny Rollins, a sax player who worked in the quintet codirected by Brownie and drummer Max Roach and who had his own troubles with drugs, would say, "Clifford was a profound influence on my personal life. He showed that it was possible to live a good, clean life and still be a good jazz musician."

The day after the accident, Dizzy Gillespie's big band was playing at Harlem's Apollo Theater. Saxophonist Benny Golson, who worked alongside Brown in Lionel Hampton's orchestra, remembered that evening only too well. The first show ended, and the musicians were preparing to return for the second set when someone ran onstage crying, calling out that Clifford Brown had been killed in a car accident the day before, along with his wife and the pianist Richie Powell. The stage director wanted the show to go on, but no one could play. The tears wouldn't let them.

In memory of the man, Golson offered to compose a kind of requiem, "trying to get a melody that would be reminiscent of [Clifford] and the way he played... I was very moody while composing this song because with each note I wrote, I realized that it was to someone who had gone – my friend forever." On July 6, 1957, Dizzy Gillespie's big band played their version of "I Remember Clifford" for the Newport festival-goers. Gillespie took a moving solo backed up by the sumptuous and melancholy orchestration by Golson, recorded by Verve Records for *Dizzy Gillespie at Newport.*

In 1955, the death of Charlie Parker launched producers and promoters into a frantic quest for the next Bird. A year later, Clifford Brown's disappearance sent them scrambling for the next Brownie. As Bob Blumenthal put it in his preface to the boxed set *The Complete Blue Note Lee Morgan Fifties Sessions*, in the same way that saxophonist Julian "Cannonball" Adderley benefited from Parker's demise, Morgan was the first to enjoy the added attention paid to emerging musicians after Brown passed.

And so it went that, playing with Gillespie's band at barely 18 years old, Morgan entered the prestigious stable of Blue Note Records. Less than a week after having him sign a contract, Alfred Lion, the label's founder, brought Morgan to Rudy Van Gelder's studio in the living room of the family home in Hackensack, New Jersey. The results of the session would be released under the title *Lee Morgan Indeed!* Morgan would go on to cut no fewer than 25 records under his name in 15 years, including six before the year 1958 was out. And that's not counting the many sessions as a sideman and the posthumous releases. That accounts for some oddities in his recording history. For example, the piece "I Remember Clifford" recorded in March 1957, a few months before the version with Diz's big band, with Lee leading a group featuring Golson on saxophone, later came out on a disc laconically titled *Lee Morgan, vol. 3*.

He became Alfred Lion's favorite, and soon he was a habitué of Van Gelder's studio, where he played alongside organist Jimmy Smith and saxophonists Hank Mobley, John Coltrane, Tina Brooks, and Johnny Griffin, all under contract with Blue Note. Morgan also appeared on his colleagues' records with other companies, and he toured incessantly with Gillespie. Diz gave him and his entire brass section colleagues bent-bell trumpets, the trade mark of be-bop's founder. We should not underestimate the influence of Diz, who made Morgan his heir apparent. In *To Be or Not to Bop*, Gillespie's autobiography, Paul West described the younger man as "almost like a baby Dizzy." There was something "very cocky and very happy-go-lucky and very comical" about him. His playing had personality; it wasn't just exercises. And when you listened, you heard it, how the relationship between Dizzy and Lee was like master and student.

During those years, Clifford Brown's influence on Morgan is as audible as Roy Eldridge's on the young Dizzy Gillespie or Fats Navarro's on Brown at the beginning of his career. In jazz as in literature, let's not forget Rod Serling's comment about developing a style by imitating someone who already has one. Lee Morgan was aware of that. He worked to create a voice by following in his idol's footsteps, in hopes of finding his own true sound later on.

Playwright Samuel B. Harps III was right to put these words in his protagonist's mouth (renamed Lee Morris to avoid legal trouble). This is in the very first scene of *Don't Explain*, while speaking of Clifford Brown:

*So, he stood like Zeus on his mountain, and he ripped
off bout five, six quick riffs in a row... sent this woman
in the front row into a motherfuckin' frenzy. Since he
had them hanging out there in that G# anyway, he said,
fuck it... I might as well blow their brains out... so... he
sucked in about three minutes of air... and he let out this
Bb... and it hung out there...*

The description of Brown's style holds up just as well
for Morgan's. As proof, give a listen to his contribution
to John Coltrane's very first classic, *Blue Train*, from
September 1957. At that point in his career, Trane had not
yet become a demigod of the avant-garde, a status that he
earned through his work in the 1960s. Fired in the spring,
along with drummer Philly Joe Jones, by Miles Davis who
was irritated by his erratic behavior, Coltrane miraculously
freed himself of heroin and alcohol. He joined Thelonious
Monk's quartet in residence at the Five Spot and discovered
spiritual revelation through his marriage to Naima Grubbs
and conversion to Islam. At Van Gelder's studio, Trane
brought together a dream quintet for his one and only
session for Blue Note as leader. The members were his
old comrade-in-arms Philly Joe Jones on drums, Paul
Chambers on bass, Kenny Drew on piano, Curtis Fuller on
trombone... and Lee Morgan. In an interview with Swedish
radio three years later, Coltrane called *Blue Train* his best
record to date "because I had a great band."

And that was no exaggeration! On the title track, a
blues with an ever-changing rhythm whose melancholy
minor theme jumps over to major during the sax solo, like

on other cuts that carried the leader's signature, the group shows astonishing cohesion considering it was put together for just one session. On the only standard on the LP, "I'm Old Fashioned" by Jerome Kerr and Johnny Mercer, Lee Morgan reveals an artfulness that no one suspected was there until then. After Coltrane states the theme, backed up only by the piano until the rhythm section breaks in, languorous choruses follow one another in delicate fashion. First Trane, then Fuller, then Drew. When it's his turn, Mogie lets fly with a salvo of stuttering notes, kneaded from the blues, with a feeling of fragility that continues until the poignant reiteration of the beginning theme.

As Tom Perchard points out in *Lee Morgan: His Life, Music and Culture*, Morgan's playing seems fiery when listened to the first time, but little by little we can hear the expression of melancholy tied to the phrasing, as well as the opposition between the pyrotechnic explosions and the uncertainty in other passages, which even his exuberance can't conceal. Of course, the ambiguity between jubilation and melancholy is part of the gospel music that his sister Ernestine played on the organ every Sunday, and those qualities are also present in the blues that ran through bebop – the two essential musical forms that Mogie grew up with.

In an interview he gave Don DeMichael from the magazine *DownBeat* in 1961, Morgan used simple, eloquent terms to describe the hell-bent nature that underpinned the way the traditional bluesmen played. There's no use celebrating existence unless you accompany it with a clear awareness of your impending end:

You know, Clifford and John Coltrane are so much alike – such a wealth of ideas and command of their instruments. Every time I heard Clifford, and now when I hear Trane, I get the impression that the doctor told them, "You've got to play everything you know today because you won't get a chance tomorrow."

On stage, in the studio, and in life, Mogie seemed to be following the motto *Carpe diem*, which is credited to the Roman poet Horace – not the hard bop pianist Horace Silver. To quote a writer who was more his contemporary, the trumpeter had the same attitude as Albert Camus, who believed that the greatest act of generosity to the future is to give everything to the present moment.

Early in January 1958, Gillespie had to dismantle his big band for financial reasons. At the time, Lee Morgan's star was at its zenith. Admitted for the upcoming fall term to the prestigious Juilliard School of Music, he moved in with his friends Spanky DeBrest and Bobby Timmons, the piano player for the Jazz Messengers. But at the end of the summer, Morgan decided to join Blakey's group and gave up on the formal training that Juilliard was ready to offer him. With this premier hard bop group, he experienced his first golden age as an artist. Tired of the mediocre conditions that most nightclubs proposed, Blakey went looking for better venues for his group, both at home and abroad. At one point, the Messengers were playing Pittsburgh's Midway Lounge, and George Pitts of the *Pittsburgh Courier* wrote, "Blakey now has one of the best groups around the circuit, with the addition of young trumpeter Lee Morgan, one of the toughest of the tough." The end of October marked the start of the sessions for the Blue Note label that would produce a number of ground-breaking albums. First came the emblematic *Moanin'*, followed by *Drums Around the Corner*, *A Night in Tunisia*, *Like Someone in Love*, and the list goes on...

Morgan took the time to record *Benny Golson and the Philadelphians* with his old friend. Then he packed his bags for two months with the Messengers in France. They were given a welcome worthy of the crème de la crème of American jazz. They triumphed at the Olympia, and their show at the theater was immortalized on record. They graced the cover of the magazine *Jazz Hot*, and Morgan was interviewed by well-known journalist François Postif. Then the Messengers turned their talents to recording the soundtrack for the thriller *The Road to Shame*, directed by Édouard Molinaro. Their tour of the French provinces and nearby countries (Netherlands, Belgium, Germany, and Switzerland) lasted until Christmas.

The next year, 1959, kept the ball rolling. The group moved between the clubs and the recording studio, most often the one run by Rudy Van Gelder, who in July moved his set-up from Hackensack to Englewood Cliffs, both in New Jersey. Benny Golson left the Messengers at the end of January, and Hank Mobley, one of the first saxophonists to have played with the group, replaced him. Mobley and Morgan got along well and complemented each other, as shown by the records they made together, whether under one person's name or the other's. Still, Mogie lobbied for Wayne Shorter to rejoin the group on tenor sax. In August his wish was granted, a few days after the New York recording for the soundtrack of another French film, *Les liaisons dangereuses 1960* by Roger Vadim (which was released in 1961 in the USA, sometimes with the title *Dangerous Love Affairs*). For the job, the Franco-American saxophonist Barney Wilen was hired. The French writer Boris Vian, something of a cult figure, made a brief on-screen appearance in this daring version of the classic epistolary novel from the eighteenth century by Pierre Choderlos de Laclos.

With his insatiable desire to play, Lee Morgan was on every stage. The afternoon following a session with Quincy Jones' big band for the recording of *The Great Wide World of Quincy Jones* that would be issued by Mercury Records on November 10, he was putting down tracks for *Introducing Wayne Shorter* for the Vee-Jay label. Blakey and Shorter had to sprint over to join Blakey and the other Messengers for an evening session to record *Africaine* that, paradoxically, would not be released until 1979. Pianist Bobby Timmons left the group in early autumn, but he and Morgan continued to share an apartment. Business was going so well that they decided to buy themselves a piano.

Like the previous year, Blakey touched down in Paris with his troupe in mid-November as part of a five-week European tour. During the trip, on December 18, saxophonist Barney Wilen and pianist Bud Powell, an expatriate in Paris for some time by then, joined the group on the stage of the Théâtre des Champs-Élysées. It was a true musical summit, but the promoters had promised better: a big-band format with not only the Messengers and Wilen, but also star French pianist Martial Solal.

Back in the States just in time for Christmas, the Jazz Messengers hit the road soon after. On New Year's Eve, Lee Morgan and his colleagues were playing the Regal Theater in Chicago, warming up for Miles Davis' group. After the concert, the two trumpet players who knew each other from the Tuesday evening improv workshops in Philadelphia went to the Sutherland Hotel to check out the local scene.

In the lobby of the chic establishment, a splendid young Asian woman attracted Morgan's eye, and, charmer that he was, he addressed her in the language of Molière. Once she and her girlfriends were sitting at a table with Miles and Mogie, the charm machine went into high gear. Kiko Yamamoto earned her living as a model and a performer with the Keigo Imperial Japanese Dancers that performed essentially in and around the Windy City, where she had recently settled. Born on the California farm of a Japanese-American family who had been interned in a camp during World War II, Kiko loved music, and jazz most of all. It looked like love at first sight between her and Mogie.

"I can't stand her," Lee told Miles jokingly, just loud enough so Kiko could hear him.

"Then it means you must like her," Miles replied.

When Blakey and his men returned to Chicago the following week for a gig, this time at the Sutherland Hotel, Lee Morgan got back in touch with Yamamoto. He would soon dedicate a piece to her, "Yama," on the album *A Night in Tunisia* with Art Blakey & the Jazz Messengers on the Blue Note label in 1960. Their love at first sight soon led to a wedding at the Bronx City Hall, while the Messengers were playing a two-week stint at the Birdland club. "Bobby

Timmons was the best man," the young Mrs. Morgan would remember later. "And then he [Morgan] went to Birdland afterward." The reception took place at the club, and everything happened so fast that none of the family members from either side attended the wedding.

She did not go on tour with him, but Kiko got to know her man as someone who was as affectionate and attentive after the wedding as during the courtship. He gave her a poodle they called Kozo and proudly introduced her to the major figures of the jazz world. In "How He Proposed," an article commissioned by *Tan*, a women's magazine published by the editors of the Afrocentrist monthly *Ebony*, Kiko Morgan was quite frank. Lee would not have married her, she said, if she had been white. The conditions in the United States were such that mixed marriages between Blacks and whites were impractical. The tensions would have distracted him from his work.

Obsessed with music, Morgan learned a lot at Art Blakey's side. The drummer taught him how to win over and hold an audience, how to get them eating out of the palm of his hand, and how to carry them, through music, from paroxysm to apotheosis, leaving them exhausted and calling for more. Blakey was also responsible for Lee Morgan's first experiences with dope. According to biographer Tom Perchard, when Morgan and Bobby Timmons joined the Jazz Messengers, Blakey predicted to them that he'd make junkies out of them within two weeks. A notorious and unrepentant heroin user, Blakey had developed a perverse strategy; he offered his musicians dope, then deducted its cost from their pay. But if heroin compromised a musician's performance, he would fire him.

At the beginning, Kiko knew nothing about her husband's dependency, but she soon discovered the secret. His peers held him in high esteem. His public adored him. He had plenty of work as leader or sideman. His many studio sessions and compositions generated sizable revenues – but he never seemed to be able to make ends meet. When she considered her husband's money problems and his frequent absences, never justified, Kiko quickly understood that her dream of leaving behind their ratty East Village apartment would never come true, not if all their savings went to financing his habit.

Kiko confided to Jeffrey S. McMillan, the author of *DelightfuLee*:

> It was really a bad addiction for him. Some people, like Art for instance… Art always controlled it, you know. It never really took over his life. Art was able to work and do whatever else he had to do. Lee wasn't like that. He was not a functioning drug addict. At first, yes, but as he got more involved with it, it just became impossible.

Blakey soon fired him. Penniless, Morgan went back to Philadelphia to live with his mother and with Kiko. Contrary to some claims, he did not use his return to his family home to fight his dependency, but to slip more completely into it. His wife tried in vain to appeal to her mother-in-law to help her, but she unjustly accused Kiko of being responsible for her son's addiction. Since love affairs generally end badly, especially when drugs are involved, Kiko Morgan finally left her husband in the summer of 1961 and traveled back to Chicago, where she found work as a model and a bunny at the Playboy Club. And who could blame her? For most people who knew him, Lee Morgan was the perfect example of what people on the street called a "greasy junkie," the kind who would sell his mother for a fix. In his book, McMillan tells about one night when he and Chet Baker went looking to buy heroin together. As soon as Baker turned his back, Morgan slipped water into his dose and kept it for himself.

Love affairs generally end badly. But when it comes to Lee Morgan, you haven't seen anything yet.

Just wait for Act II.

~

In 1967, three years after proving that he wasn't dead yet with the record *The Sidewinder* (Blue Note, 1964), one of the most emblematic and popular albums of the hard bop era, Lee Morgan did not even have an instrument of his own. He hocked his horn and even his winter coat to pay for dope. And even if he'd had a trumpet in his hands, he was so messed up he wouldn't have been able to play it. One frigid night, Lee Morgan would meet the woman who would save his career and his life, before ending both of them.

A native of Shallotte in North Carolina, the woman who would one day call herself Helen Morgan (even if she and Lee never tied the knot) had a habit of taking in jazz artists on their way down. Among them were more than a few junkies. Once the clubs closed, "Helen's Place" was where a man could get warm and always find something to eat. On one particularly cold night, that was where Mogie found a spot. "Child, you need a coat," were the first words she supposedly spoke to the barely human form slumped on the sidewalk, so pitiful that the woman's heart "just smiled on him." She had abandoned the children she had as a teenager, and maybe she was trying to redeem herself by coming to the rescue of forsaken souls. One thing's for sure: what happened between her and Morgan is the stuff of tragedy.

In 1991, 20 years after Helen murdered him, the original production of the play *Don't Explain* ran for four months at the Nuyorican Poets Café, just steps away from the former club where the trumpeter died. Ominously, the place was called Slugs. Samuel B. Harps III's musical drama earned seven AUDELCO Awards, given out annually to promote the creativity within the African American community. The play tells the story of the Lee Morgan tragedy, and Billie Holiday's title song provides the leitmotif. Written by Lady Day along with the pianist Arthur Herzog Jr., the song is told through the voice of a woman who is cheated on, but who prefers that her flighty lover keep his silence rather than offer lies unworthy of him. Helen Merrill's poignant 1954 recording of the standard features a flamboyant performance by Clifford Brown.

When the play was first staged, Harps was in his early 30s, Lee Morgan's age in February 1972. In an interview with Karl Stark for the *Philadelphia Inquirer* in January 1992, Harps said he composed his play like a piece of music. He identified the pauses between the dialogues as beats, with the action accompanied by trumpet and piano interludes composed by trumpeter Roy Hargrove, a contemporary heir of Morgan's who died prematurely in the fall of 2018. Harps cautioned his audience not to see *Don't Explain* as a jazz show. "People don't have to like jazz to like my plays. It's really a love story. Jazz is just the icing on the cake."

They don't have to like the music, he was saying. But it helps if they do.

In the tradition of classical tragedy, the fate of Lee Morris (played by the poet Ron Cephas Jones in the play's first staging) has been determined before the curtain goes up. The author takes some liberties with the facts now and again, but he maintains that the disastrous love affair between Lee and Elana (the name he gives the character who represents Helen) is based strictly on the truth, from the idyllic night they meet at Slugs to the bloody outcome at the same place. Harps had originally decided to write a play based on what he had read about the trumpeter and his music, but that turned out to be harder than he thought.

First of all, he had a problem. His character was a wife-beating junkie, and he had to do something to lift him out of the swamp. He gave him an incandescent poetic energy, the verbal equivalent of Morgan's intense trumpet style. Some of his soliloquies sound like the man's incendiary improvisation style.

> When I'm there on stage, I feel suspended. Like my spirit is sitting in the front row wit' a Scotch and water in one hand and a cigarette in the other, checkin' my ass out. I can close my eyes, and see the whole world, and not hear a sound.

Here, we are close to the idea put forward by LeRoi Jones (alias Amiri Bakara) in *Blues People*. According to him, heroin was popular among Black musicians, especially those of the be-bop and hard bop generations, because it turned the sense of social exclusion felt by African Americans into a kind of advantage.

The documentary *I Called Him Morgan*, written and directed for Netflix by Kasper Collin in 2017, echoes, but also completes, Samuel Harps' stage tragedy. The Swedish documentary director has a definite interest in jazz and its tragic characters. Ten years earlier, he filmed the life of saxophonist Albert Ayler in *My Name Is Albert Ayler* (2007). *Jazz Times* dubbed the film "one of the most starkly beautiful and moving documentaries ever made about a jazz musician."

In his film, Collin calls to the witness stand the many musicians who knew Lee Morgan and Helen Moore well. Among them are composers and sax players Wayne Shorter, Billy Harper, and Bennie Maupin; bassists Larry Ridley, Jymie Merritt, and Paul West; and drummer Charles Persip, the latter two having worked with Mogie in Gillespie's big band. Their testimonies give us an idea of Morgan's lightning rise to fame, the depth of his talent, and the absurdity of the way he died.

Twelve years his elder, Helen Moore saved Morgan from the wreck that drugs had cast him into. As his common-law partner, she looked after him, fed him, spiffed him up, brought him back to a functioning state, and managed his career. In their large apartment in the Bronx, he slowly returned to being the virtuoso trumpet player he had once been, the man who used to cross horns with the great Dizzy Gillespie himself. Yet, in appreciation for all Moore had done, Morgan took a younger mistress, Judith Johnson. He went and lived with her and forgot to even send a word to his guardian angel. Humiliated, Helen went to Slugs on East 3rd Street where he was playing on February 19, 1972, the night of the Snowstorm of the Century in New York. The other woman was in the audience. In her purse, Helen carried the pistol that Morgan had given her for her protection.

"I came for the draw," she announced, according to sax player Billy Harper. It was a line that could have meant any number of things.

Morgan was determined to avoid a scene. He threw her out of the club by main force, without giving her time to put on her coat. From her purse, the pistol dropped onto the ground...

Helen picked it up out of the snow and went back into the club.

After firing at him at point blank range, she told herself it was just a bad dream.

The ambulance took forever to reach the club because of the blizzard. Forever was too late. By the time the attendants made their way into Slugs with their stretcher, Lee Morgan had bled to death in the arms of his murderess who was already in mourning.

At the heart of *I Called Him Morgan*, of course, is the title character's music and Helen Moore's voice. Twenty years after she got out of prison, she agreed to answer questions from Larry Reni Thomas, a professor from Wilmington, North Carolina, who had taught her in an adult education program. A month before she died, Helen Moore drew a candid self-portrait in her soft Southern drawl, a voice that reminds us of Billie Holiday. *Hush now, don't explain.* She talked about everything that led up to that fateful night. Then, slowly, what could have been a second trial for a killer turned into a study of contrition and forgiveness.

That's why the words of bassist Larry Ridley, Morgan's partner on *Cornbread* (Blue Note, 1967), are so essential. Not long after Helen got out on parole after two years in prison, he spotted her in the audience at a club, The Needle's Eye. Like many musicians who were outraged by what she did, he had promised himself to give her a piece of his mind if ever they crossed paths. Instead, to his great surprise, he took her in his arms and held her in a wave of emotion. "The anger just went away," he told the filmmaker.

Really, there is no reason to be astonished. After all, she was Helen Moore, the living contradiction of F. Scott Fitzgerald who claimed, "There are no second acts in American lives."

Black and Blue (II)

At the beginning of the 1960s, Black Americans were intensifying their struggle for their civil rights, and musicians found inspiration in that great social movement. On August 31, 1960, almost three years to the day before Martin Luther King spoke of his dream at the foot of the Lincoln Memorial, drummer Max Roach summoned a hand-picked group of musicians into the studio for the first of two recording sessions that produced his famous *Freedom Now Suite*. The piece was the fruit of work begun a year earlier with lyricist Oscar Brown. Inspired by the Emancipation Proclamation pronounced by Abraham Lincoln and African anticolonial and independence movements, the album *We Insist!* incorporates a number of elements from avant-garde jazz, which was emerging at the time. There was no piano, for example, and slogans were chanted in the piece "Protest," along with passages of collective improvisation in "Tears for Johannesburg." The album's principal theme was the struggles of Black people around the world.

This manifesto was praised as a major work in the *Penguin Guide to Jazz*, and to complete it, Max Roach recruited Abbey Lincoln, a regular bandmate of his, whom he would marry in 1962. At the time, she was better known as a smoldering singer of sentimental ballads. But that changed. The woman who was nicknamed "Marilyn Monroe in sepia" stepped forward as a politically involved artist and one of the major voices in the civil rights movement. Expanding the band, Roach turned to veteran sax player Coleman Hawkins ("Driva Man") and Nigerian percussionist Babatunde Olatunji, one of the main artists behind the integration of African rhythms into American jazz ("All Africa," "Tears for Johannesburg"). Composed as a response to the Sharpeville Massacre perpetrated by South Africa's apartheid regime, the fifth and last piece ("Tears for Johannesburg") is the high point of the album. According to Nat Hentoff, that piece sums up everything the players and singers of the album are trying to communicate. There will be no stopping the move for freedom in the US and in South Africa.

The same year, saxophonist Ornette Coleman, a leading figure of the avant-garde, launched a sixth album recorded just months after *We Insist!* That was *Free Jazz: A Collective Improvisation by the Ornette Coleman Double Quartet*. The album cover featured a fragment of a Jackson Pollock action painting (*White Light*, 1954), a natural choice for the freedom-seeking artist and songwriter of "When Will the Blues Leave?" The record brought together the regular members of Coleman's quartet (Don Cherry on pocket trumpet, Scott LaFaro on bass, and Billy Higgins on drums), augmented by multi-instrumentalist Eric Dolphy, trumpeter Freddie Hubbard, and drummer Ed Blackwell. On the one and only track, necessarily divided for the two sides of an LP, the rhythm sections play together, and though there is a succession of solos typical of jazz, the music is shot through with spontaneous outbursts by the other brass instruments that transform the music into the collective improvisation promised by the title. In that period of intense agitation in American history, free jazz is often considered an angry scream heading off into cacophony, given its rejection of the elegant tunes of cool jazz and the spirit of consensus of hard bop. Yet Coleman's music never lacks lyricism and at times sounds to us, when we step away from our first impression, strangely serene.

The year 1961 also witnessed the emergence of Horace Tapscott and his Pan Afrikan Peoples Arkestra (also known as PAPA or The Ark) on the American West Coast. The group's mission was to preserve, develop, and promote African American music. In 1963, As Tapscott, who once played trombone with the Lionel Hampton band, expanded his spiritual, political, and esthetic universe, PAPA dissolved into a wider organization, the Underground Musicians' Association (UGMA), later renamed the Union of God's Musicians and Artists Ascension (UGMAA). Over the years, the Arkestra welcomed any number of members, including saxophonists Arthur Blythe and David Murray, cornetist Butch Morris, and even drummer Stanley Crouch, better known now as the hagiographer of trumpeter Wynton Marsalis.

Though it was essentially a religious and artistic Black nationalist collective, the UGMAA was very close to another organization founded in the fall of 1966 that came to symbolize African American political radicalism – the Black Panthers. A Marxist-Leninist party that took its name from the first Black superhero to be born in the pages of Marvel Comics, in J. Edgar Hoover's words, the Black Panthers "without question, represents the great threat to the internal security of the country." The two organizations had their headquarters at the same address. "It was guns upstairs, musicians in the basement," Tapscott said later. Relations were friendly enough that Tapscott produced the album *Seize the Time* (Flying Dutchman, 1969) by Elaine Brown in UGMAA's independent studio. Brown was an author, pianist, singer, and militant and future chairman of the Panthers from 1974 to 1977. Her memoir, *A Taste of Power: A Black Woman's Story* (Anchor, 1993), would soon enjoy a screen adaptation.

The album's pièce de résistance, "The Meeting," would become the Black Panthers' hymn, with its call for the arrival of a Black messiah. "Where have you been all these years?" Brown wonders.

~

The militant attitude of African Americans during those years wasn't just the doing of the avant-garde. In 1962, encouraged by his friend and producer Norman Granz to create a "definitive early-blues feel," Montreal pianist Oscar Peterson contributed "Hymn to Freedom," his first major composition and part of his emblematic album, *Night Train* (Verve, 1962). Inspired by the Negro spirituals that illuminated the pianist's childhood in the city's Little Burgundy neighborhood, the piece soon became an ode to the civil rights movement, once Peterson and Granz agreed that the tune needed words. They turned to Malcolm Dodds, composer, arranger, and choir leader of the Malcolm Dodds Singers. He in turn looked to Harriette Hamilton, who had written most of the words to the group's original songs. "All the lyrics had to do was express in very simple language the hope for unity, peace, and dignity for mankind," Hamilton said later. "It was easy to write."

In August 1963, in the week preceding Martin Luther King's historic speech at the foot of the Lincoln Memorial, the respectable pianist Duke Ellington, composer, maestro, and icon of the swing era, created *My People* in Chicago as part of the exhibition *A Century of Negro Progress*. On the most recent CD reissue of this show recorded in front of a live audience (*Duke Ellington's My People – The Complete Show*, Storyville, 2012), we can listen to the full performance of this musical review narrated and staged by the Duke himself. The most striking cut is "King Fit the Battle of Alabam." Disgusted by the actions of Theophilus Eugene "Bull" Connor and the Birmingham police five months earlier and the brutal repression of Black militants in the streets of that city, Duke gave Martin Luther King the starring role in his rereading of the traditional "Joshua Fit the Battle of Jericho." It was an homage not only to the pastor, but also to the courageous resistance of Birmingham's Black population. In his autobiography *Music Is my Mistress* (Da Capo Press, 1976), Ellington states that he wrote the first song as a tribute to Reverend King who, after he listened to it in rehearsal, burst into tears. That is the story told by Harvey G. Cohen in *Duke Ellington's America* (University of Chicago Press, 2011). With the complete performance of *My People*, we discover a second homage to the pastor, an instrumental laconically entitled "King" that had never been included on record before, a typical Ellington swing composition, with energy and intensity that perfectly translate the determined convictions of the man it was dedicated to.

On February 12, 1964, at New York's Lincoln Center Philharmonic Hall, Miles Davis and his brand-new quintet gave a benefit concert commissioned by the NAACP, the Congress of Racial Equality, and the Student Nonviolent Coordinating Committee to support Black voter registration in Louisiana and Mississippi. Dedicated to the memory of JFK, assassinated a few months earlier, the concert would be issued on two separate discs the next year (*My Funny Valentine* and *Four & More*, Columbia, 1965). During that same month, with his Jazz Messengers, Art Blakey put out an album whose title left no doubt: *The Freedom Rider* (Blue Note, 1964). The title cut, featuring Blakey playing solo, honors the Freedom Riders, those civil rights militants who rode buses from state to state to put the Supreme Court's *Boynton v. Virginia* judgment to the test. Was segregation in interstate transport really illegal or not?

At Carnegie Hall on March 21, 1964, pianist and singer Nina Simone let fly with "Mississippi Goddam," created in white heat in less than an hour and first presented some time earlier at the Village Gate. Simone, who wrote and performed her own material, was reacting to the assassination of the NAACP's Medgar Wiley Evers on June 12, 1963 in Jackson, Mississippi, and the bombing of the 16th Street Baptist church in Birmingham that killed four people the following September 15th. Simone sarcastically introduced the song as "a show tune but the show hasn't been written for it yet." We can imagine how the majority white, upper-class audience felt as they listened to Simone speak of her state of mind:

> Alabama's gotten me so upset
> Tennessee made me lose my rest
> And everybody knows about Mississippi Goddam.

Included on an album developed from a series of concerts (*Nina Simone in Concert*, Philips, 1964), "Mississippi Goddam" was also issued as a 45 and became a standard of the civil rights movement. No surprise – the song was banned from the airwaves in most of the Southern states, the reason supposedly being the blasphemy contained in the title. Boxes of promo copies sent to the radio stations were quickly expedited back to the record company, each 45 carefully broken in two. That didn't stop Simone from performing the song the evening of March 24, 1965, on stage in front of tens of thousands of demonstrators for Black voting rights, who had taken part in the march on Selma organized by Martin Luther King.

The demonstration inspired trumpeter Blue Mitchell to embark on his own "March on Selma" on *Down With It!* (Blue Note, 1966).

~

After adopting Ornette Coleman's "Peace" on his first album as a leader (*Archie Shepp – Bill Dixon Quartet*, Savoy,

1962), sax artist Archie Shepp became John Coltrane's friend and protégé. Shepp would pay tribute to him with his record *Four for Trane* (Impulse!, 1964) and then go on to participate in the sessions that led to *A Love Supreme* (Impulse!, 1964), considered Coltrane's masterwork. Unfortunately, the tracks which Shepp contributed to would not make it onto the record, and would not be released until 2002, but his bond with the sax supreme was cemented with the issue of *Ascension* (Impulse!, 1965), where we can hear the two playing together. On *New Thing at Newport* (Impulse!, 1965), on Side A Coltrane plays an excerpt from his Newport Jazz Festival concert, while Side B features Shepp.

On *Fire Music* (Impulse!, 1965), we can feel Shepp's growing political awareness, as well as his interest in traditional African music. On that record is the piece "Malcolm, Malcolm, Semper Malcolm," a requiem for Malcolm X, assassinated February 21st of that year.

Six days before, the charismatic leader had told photographer Gordon Parks that the Nation of Islam, the group he had publicly disassociated himself from the previous year, was actively trying to eliminate him. On that February evening at the Audubon Ballroom in Manhattan, as he was about to give a speech before the Organization of Afro-American Unity, one of the 400 or so audience members rushed the stage and shot him in the chest with a sawed-off shotgun. Two other shooters broke into the theater with semi-automatic weapons. Malcolm X was pronounced dead a short time after his ambulance arrived at the Columbia Presbyterian Hospital. The autopsy stated that he had succumbed to 21 bullet wounds to his chest, left shoulder, arms, and legs.

Archie Shepp would not be the only one to honor the memory of the murdered leader. Phil Cohran was another, known primarily as the trumpet player in Chicago's Sun Ra Arkestra from 1959 to 1961, a founding member of the AACM, and inventor of the frankiphone, a sort of electrified lamellophone. In 1968, Cohran created his Artistic Heritage Ensemble. The 12 musicians included Don Myrick and Louis Satterfield (future members of Earth, Wind & Fire) and legendary guitarist Pete Cosey. The ambitious suite they played, *The Malcolm X Memorial: A Tribute in Music* (Zulu Records), remains one of the most vibrant musical portraits of the late leader, a builder of awareness and apostle of Afrocentric unity. The next year, avant-garde singer Leon Thomas and sax player Pharoah Sanders composed "Malcolm's Gone."

Archie Shepp's subsequent albums would transmit his increasingly militant politics. *Attica Blues* (Impulse!, 1972) found inspiration in the riots at Attica prison after George Jackson, writer and member of the Black Panther Party, was murdered by guards there. *The Cry of my People* (Impulse!, 1972), whose title carries echoes of Ellington, needs no further commentary.

In 1965, it wasn't just Shepp's music that was incendiary. Despite the Civil Rights Act of 1964 that in theory signaled the end of racial segregation, discrimination lived on and the situation exploded in Watts, the Los Angeles ghetto. The day after three members of a Black family were arrested, the neighborhood caught fire. The riots that followed were among the most violent in American history. "Burn, baby, burn!" the rioters shouted. The ghetto was set afire, torn apart, pillaged. Some 30 people died and a thousand were injured. But it was only the beginning. On July 28, 1967, after an altercation between white policemen and a Black taxi driver, the ghetto in Newark, New Jersey, was burned. The riots soon spread to Detroit: 43 dead and 400 injured. The long hot summer provided more than 159 race riots and 83 deaths.

With this explosive atmosphere and the emergence of new leaders in the Black community, Martin Luther King's popularity was on the decline, among African Americans and the population as a whole. Curiously, the decline seemed to have started with him winning the Nobel Peace Prize on October 14, 1964. In 1966, a Gallup poll showed that two-thirds of Americans had an unfavorable opinion of him. His anti-Vietnam War stance increased that tendency, and he was also criticized for his support of the federal War on Poverty. Already King had his share of enemies, and he was making new ones, some very powerful. In Memphis, on April 3, 1968, the day before he was murdered, he was perfectly candid in his last speech and did not shy away from the dangers he was facing. He might not make it to the promised land, though that did not matter, as long as his people did.

At the Westbury Music Fair on Long Island, three days after King was shot down on the balcony of the Lorraine Motel, Nina Simone sang "Why? (The King of Love Is Dead)," written by her bassist Gene Taylor. The piece ran nearly 15 minutes and featured Simone's sermonizing. A shorter version appeared on 'Nuff Said! (RCA Victor, 1968), an album that included a remake of "Backlash Blues," a protest song based on a Langston Hughes poem.

The day after the assassination, musical tributes to King began to pour in. Saxophonist Cecil Payne opened his *Zodiac* with a requiem simply called "Martin Luther King." For reasons that escape me, the record did not come out until 1973 on the Strata-East label. Pianist and composer Mary Lou Williams dedicated two pieces to King: "Tell Him Not to Talk Too Long" and "I Have a Dream." The first composition appeared on her famous album *Mary Lou's Mass*.

In the spring of 1969, pianist and composer Herbie Hancock launched his seventh and last album for Blue Note, *The Prisoner*. It was designed as "a social statement written in music" dedicated to the martyr. The first track was called "I Have a Dream." First created in 1968 for a concert at the University of California Jazz Festival, the piece expresses "how Black people have been imprisoned" throughout American history. Another piece, "Firewater," composed by bassist Buster Williams, represents "the social duality of the oppressor and the oppressed: the fire symbolizes the heat in violence and abuse of power," whereas water refers to King's pacifism. The title of "He Who Lives in Fear" is a tribute to the pastor who "had to live in an atmosphere charged with intimidation."

In October of the same year, sax player and composer Oliver Nelson also recorded an album dedicated to King, *Black, Brown and Beautiful* (Flying Dutchman, 1970). It expresses anger, yes, but is also an act of exploration with many contemplative passages.

The year 1970 saw Max Roach record a posthumous duo with King: he accompanied the "I Have a Dream" speech with a drum improvisation on Chattahoochee Red, Columbia.

In the speech he gave to open the 1964 Berlin Jazz Festival, Martin Luther King made a clear connection between jazz and the strength of the civil rights movement. "Jazz speaks for life," he said. Take the hardships of life and put them into music, and you will emerge with a sense of hope and triumph. And indeed, this was triumphant music.

There's no doubt that MLK loved jazz deeply. For him it was universal. And jazz loved him back.

Almost Blue

The high-contrast black-and-white image shows a noisy enthusiastic crowd applauding and cheering the artist who is talking to them in a lazy drawl. A junkie's voice.

"Well, we've come to that time in the evening when there's not much time left. The song is called 'Almost Blue' and we'd appreciate it if you could kind of try to be quiet 'cause it's *that* type of tune, you know…"

Here we are, at the end of the reception celebrating the premiere of *Broken Noses*, a mid-length boxing documentary made by photographer and filmmaker Bruce Weber. The picture opened at the 1987 Cannes Film Festival. By that time, Chet, whose music was featured in the film, had only a passing resemblance to that excessively photogenic young star portrayed time and time again by his friend William Claxton. Thirty years earlier, Claxton had immortalized Baker's god-like beauty.

Off screen, pianist Frank Strazzeri launches into the melancholy intro of the contemporary standard penned by Elvis Costello. Chet is sitting on a stool, trumpet in one hand, mike in the other. Seeing the close up of his face, a parchment of ordeals and excesses, you would think he was 20 years older than his true age of 58. In the midst of a nest of deep wrinkles, his closed eyes are like two small abysses beneath his brows.

As the evening and the film come to their conclusion, he whispers the painfully beautiful lines that Costello wrote:

Almost blue
Almost doing things we used to do
There's a girl here and she's almost you
Almost

As a joke, I suppose, a lady friend told me she was a little disappointed I had her watch *Let's Get Lost*, Bruce Weber's dreamy documentary that tells the up and down story of the life and career of the singer and trumpet player. She had always pictured Baker as a romantic hero. Not that she had any illusions about the young man with the horn, whose death, as nebulous as it was tragic, granted him iconic status like his contemporaries James Dean and Marilyn Monroe. If we are to believe my friend Annie, when you are a fan, sometimes it's better not to know certain details about our idols' lives. And I do sympathize with her, especially since Weber draws a lucid, frontal portrait of the artist as a fallen angel of cool jazz.

Let's Get Lost opens on the beaches of Santa Monica in the spring of 1987. The film alternates between sequences from the last months of Chet Baker's life and archival footage from his beginnings in the 1950s, when he played alongside giants like saxmen Charlie Parker and Gerry Mulligan and his pianist Russ Freeman. The film takes its title from the standard written by Frank Loesser and Jimmy McHugh and first sung by Mary Martin in Curtis Bernhardt's comedy *Happy Go Lucky*. Baker recorded it 12 years later for *Chet Baker Sings and Plays* (Pacific). It was the first LP Bruce Weber bought when he was a teenager in Pittsburgh.

Chesney Henry Baker Jr., nicknamed Chet, came into this world in Yale, Oklahoma, on December 23, 1929, and grew up in Glendale, California. His family moved there when he was ten. Radio announcer, semi-professional guitar and banjo player who strummed country music, Chesney Sr. gave his son a trombone as a gift. That might have been the father's way of saying he was sorry for the beatings he inflicted on his wife Vera and his son, on certain nights when he had a few too many and the burden of living got too heavy. Young Chet would soon trade the trombone for a trumpet out of admiration for Harry James. James played a jazzy style of variety tunes, expressionistic and grandiloquent, the very opposite of the way Chet would end up sounding. As a teenager, he began playing in dance bands and got passionate about Lester Young, precursor to the kind of cool jazz that Chet would go on to champion. He enlisted in the armed forces, and, as a trumpeter for the 2980 Army Band stationed in Berlin in 1946, he discovered be-bop as played by Dizzy Gillespie and Charlie Parker, as well as contemporary white orchestras led by Woody Herman and Stan Kenton.

Discharged two years later, he briefly studied harmony and music theory at El Camino College in Los Angeles but sought refuge in the Army again in 1950 after an unhappy love affair. While by himself, he worked at imitating the phrasing and reproducing the smooth melodic lines and minimalist approach of Miles Davis from his *Birth of the Cool* period. During his first stay in Paris, Baker raved about Davis in an interview with *Jazz Magazine* journalist Daniel Filipacchi, who played Davis' "Blue Haze" for him. "That's my man," he said. "I'd listen to him from morning til night. Miles is a genius. All I can say is that's the only style I like. I want to play like that." In an interview with *DownBeat* a few years before his death, he admitted that he could never have found his voice on the trumpet if he hadn't listened to Miles.

Around that time, Chet Baker began attending jam sessions where he played opposite saxophonists Dexter Gordon and Paul Desmond. At the Blackhawk club one night, as he joined pianist Dave Brubeck on stage, he noticed a young fan who was entranced by the music: future actor and director Clint Eastwood.

Sentenced to be disciplined by the military, Chet chose to desert and was finally discharged, judged to have a personality incompatible with Army life. In 1952, he met up with two renowned sax players. First was Stan Getz, who quickly developed a dislike for this gifted but primitive trumpeter. Getz saw in him little more than a pretty boy unworthy of the popular success that seemed to follow him from the start. Charlie Parker was another story. He picked Baker from among a cohort of young California players to accompany him on a West Coast tour from Los Angeles to Vancouver, contributing to the legend essentially created by Baker himself. Some jazz historians attribute his addiction to heroin to his stint with Parker. No surprise there. A lot of young musicians figured all they needed to do was shoot up to reach Bird's level of genius.

That same year, Chet joined baritone sax player Gerry Mulligan's quartet, one of the rare ones without a piano, and he soon reached star status. Every Monday night, Mulligan and Chet held court at The Haig, where chic Angelinos hung out and listened to music. Directors and big screen stars, Jane Russell and Marilyn Monroe to name just two, liked the atmosphere. The duo had the crowd buzzing with their mix of original pieces composed by Mulligan and tried and true standards. One was "My Funny Valentine," and no performance by Chet was complete without it, on trumpet or sung, or sometimes both. How did he manage to turn this syrupy Rodgers and Hart ballad into a tragic, somber ode to a love condemned to fade away? No one had the answer, not even Mulligan, who had chosen the song from the musical *Babes in Arms*. "I think Chet was kind of a freak talent," the baritone player would say years later, admitting there was no way for him to know about Chet's abilities or where they came from.

Everything was going great for the group. They had an all but permanent residency at The Haig until Mulligan got busted for possession and use of narcotics in the summer of 1953. For the remaining weeks of the contract, Stan Getz replaced the jailed baritone despite the former's disdain for Chet. Any musical dialogue between equals was impossible at the time due to the trumpeter's lack of skill. But no matter! Richard Bock, boss and producer of the Pacific label, believed he had found in Chet the living symbol of West Coast cool jazz. Leading a combo directed, in reality, by pianist Russ Freeman, Chet Baker triumphed on stage and on record, singing and playing trumpet, the epitome of a musical style that was airy and light, sunny and contemplative.

In a place as obsessed with image as Hollywood, the pictures of him taken by his friend William Claxton soon turned Chet into the "James Dean of jazz." Historian David Gelly, author of the work *Icons of Jazz: A History in Photographs 1900-2000*, sees Baker as "James Dean, Sinatra, and Bix, rolled into one." A good number of women in the audience came less to hear him and more to get an eyeful. While married to his first wife Charlaine Souder, Chet had a way of disappearing with lady admirers during the break. "He was fucking everything in sight, treating Charlaine like a piece of shit," his drummer Larry Bunker told biographer James Gavin, author of *Deep in a Dream: The Long Night of Chet Baker* (2002). "Balling chicks on the ten-minute break out in the car while Charlaine was sitting in the club. That was his style."

Chet cut endless records in all formats for Pacific Jazz: as a quartet, sextet, septet, or with a string orchestra. His bandmates included the most prestigious musicians from the American West Coast: saxmen Bud Shanks, Zoot Sims, Jack Montrose, and Bob Cooper; bassists Leroy Vinnegar and Howard Rumsey; drummers Max Roach and Shelley Manne. In 1955, Hollywood offered Chet his first small role. He played Jockey, the trumpet player on the Okinawa base in *Hell's Horizon*, a war story written and directed by Tom Gries. Despite receiving some appealing film proposals, he would not return to the set, preferring the musician's life to the actor's.

Named trumpeter of the year in 1954 in all the American

jazz magazines (much to the dismay of Miles Davis, who considered the winner to have shamelessly plagiarized his style), Chet Baker went from one success to the next as he worked on and refined his idealized playboy image. With the generous paychecks he cashed, he bought his first cars, and he would hang on to his collection until the end. And he continued using heroin compulsively, which earned him repeated run-ins with the authorities and his first arrests.

In the fall of 1955 he signed with the French label Barclay. In October, he began recording Bob Zieff compositions with his group. When his pianist Dick Twardzik died of an overdose in his hotel room, Chet decided to soldier on with the tour and ignore Twardzik's parents' accusations. He stayed on out of love for a woman named Liliane Rovère whom Alain Gerber mentions in his writings about Chet. The longer stay also gave him the opportunity to work with a large number of new musicians, mostly French.

Back in the USA early in 1956, he toured the East Coast before returning to Los Angeles. There, for the Pacific label, he recorded *The Route* and *Playboys* (also known as *Picture of Heath*). At his side was sax player Art Pepper, also a notorious junkie. By then divorced from Charlaine, Chet married Halema, the lovely Pakistani woman who appeared in some of William Claxton's glamorous photos. She gave birth to a son in 1957, Chesney Aftab, but raising a child was not a primary concern for Chet. That summer, his heroin habit became more intense, and he was arrested again on narcotics charges. In 1958, he signed with Riverside and made several albums with the label, including the excellent *Chet* with Bill Evans on piano and Philly Joe Jones on drums.

Baker lived in Europe from 1959 to 1964 and received a better welcome there than in his own country. Chet handed off his wife and child to sculptor Peter Broome, the brother of an old high school friend who was also an expatriate in Paris. Broome was disgusted by Baker's inability to assume his paternal responsibilities and ended up looking after the boy himself. Halema found herself involved in Chet's legal troubles, against her will. She was raising Chesney Aftab on her own, far from the boy's father and certainly without his moral and financial support. Chet might have figured he could save face by dedicating a song to the boy ("Chetty's Lullaby"), but he never once sang it to him in person.

On one long, endless tour, in 1961 Chet met the woman who would be his third wife, British actress Carol Ann Jackson. The couple was constantly hounded by the paparazzi, and his legal woes were front-page news. He was expelled from Germany and England, then jailed for several months in Italy. All the same, even more than in Hollywood, "Chet the Americano" was a shining star. He appeared on the big screen with Adriano Celentano and the buxom German beauty Elke Sommer (another of my teenage mistakes) in *Urlatori alla sbarra*, a comedy directed by Lucio Fulci who did everything in his power to promote the Americano's Italian career. Of the records Baker made during that period, the best may be *Chet Is Back!* (RCA, 1962, also known as *The Italian Sessions*). The trumpeter was in fine form and working with the crème de la crème of European jazzmen: from Belgium, Bobby Jaspar and René Thomas on sax and guitar; from Italy, Amedeo Tommasi on piano; the Frenchman Benoît Quersin on bass; and from Switzerland, Daniel Humair on drums.

Baker returned to the United States in 1965 and cut a series of credible LPs for Prestige whose present participle titles echoed the classic sides made for the same label ten years earlier by Miles Davis: *Smokin'*, *Groovin'*, *Comin' On*, *Cool Burnin'*, and *Boppin'*. A number of other commercial recordings followed that are of little interest for jazz fans. Produced with the outfit The Mariachi Brass, the albums are an attempt to reproduce the success of jazz-pop trumpeter and singer Herb Alpert, at the head of his Tijuana Brass. The project fell flat. The British invasion was in full swing, and Chet wasn't drawing crowds. He was having trouble finding gigs, and then things went from bad to worse. One evening in 1966, while Chet was leaving the Trident restaurant in Sausalito, on San Francisco Bay, after a concert, a gang of thugs working for a dealer with a grudge beat him up. They broke his jaw and knocked out almost all his front teeth. Art imitates life. The incident was repeated in Spike Lee's *Mo' Better Blues* (1990) when trumpeter Bleek Gilliam gets his face rearranged in the alley behind the Beneath the Underdog club.

Unable to play, Chet entered a long dry spell. He did all kinds of odd jobs a lot less glamorous than what his pretty-boy looks and musical talent had accustomed him to – pumping gas, for example. After several years of trying to learn how to play trumpet with false teeth, he climbed back on stage in 1973, physically diminished and somewhat pitiful. His old success was just a memory, especially in the United States, where he was considered a has-been. No wonder that a standard like "You Can't Go Home Again," a nostalgic lament for the paradises lost, found a spot in his repertory. The song lent its title to an album for A&M, the label founded by Herb Alpert.

The years brought a long and painful descent into decadence, the twilight of an idol. The process lasted a decade and a half and did feature a few memorable moments. There were on-stage and on-record reunions with old companions (sax players Gerry Mulligan and Paul Desmond) and encounters with new ones (among others, pianists Michel Graillier, Alain Jean-Marie, and Enrico Pieranunzi; guitarist Philip Catherine; bassists Charlie Haden, Niels-Henning Ørsted Pedersen, and Riccardo Del Fra).

Among the highlights for Baker during this period, there was the meeting with the British singer-composer-songwriter Declan Patrick MacManus – alias Elvis Costello. The Briton was an old fan of Chet's. His song "Almost Blue," inspired by the standard "The Thrill Is Gone," was featured on *Chet Baker Sings* (Pacific, 1954). The latter song is not to be mistaken for B. B. King's blues of the same name. In 1983, Costello invited Baker to improvise on a track for his album *Punch the Clock*, the piece "Shipbuilding" (Columbia). These occasional forays made it possible for a new and younger audience to discover the "ex-James Dean of cool jazz."

Chet returned the favor by inviting Costello to perform with him at Ronnie Scott's, the legendary London club. Recorded June 6, 1986, the concert is available on CD and DVD. Quite the show, featuring Chet and his guests, Costello and Van Morrison, with superb accompaniment by Michel Graillier on piano and Riccardo Del Fra on bass. They revisit a number of standards, including "You

Can't Go Home Again." The DVD includes a conversation between Baker and Costello that, in a sense, prefigures the documentary film Bruce Weber would undertake the following year, in which Chet comes full circle by making "Almost Blue" his own, now part of his repertory.

~

Some 20 years Chet Baker's junior, filmmaker Bruce Weber made a name for himself at the end of the 1970s as a fashion photographer, most notably for GQ. His sultry portrait of Brazilian athlete Tomás Valdemar Hintnaus skimpily dressed for a Calvin Klein ad contributed to his fame, or notoriety. In the winter of 1986, he met Chet Baker in a New York jazz club and proposed a photo session that would also include filming for a three-minute short based on the standard "Blame it on my Youth," an emblematic piece from his repertory if ever there was one. The two men became friends, so close that Baker opened up to Weber completely. The latter then convinced him to take on a more ambitious project.

In an interview with Anne Lewis of the *Austin Chronicle* to mark the twentieth anniversary of the film, Weber was very frank. Making *Let's Get Lost* was no walk in the park, and conversations with his star were laborious. "Sometimes we'd have to stop for some reason or another and then, because Chet was a junkie and couldn't do things twice, we'd have to start all over again. But we grew to really like him," Weber described. In another interview with *Time Out*, he added, "You'd decide that, when Chet finally gets up, you'll grab him and talk to him about the early days. But when Chet gets here, and he's had a fight with his girlfriend, and he wants to record a song… So what happens is that your world becomes like a jazz suite. You have to go along with him."

To draw this larger than life portrait of Baker, Bruce Weber looked for help from those who had been close to him. Lovers, musicians he'd played with, and family members added candid testimonies about the artist and the man they had known intimately, loved passionately, or hated deeply. Though the filmmaker seems truly taken with his subject, the result is far from panegyric. His trumpeter colleague Jack Sheldon is full of praise for the instinctive sophistication of his playing, but his wife Carol and former girlfriend Ruth Young have nothing but bitterness. They describe Baker as a charming but pathological liar, an unscrupulous manipulator, a perverse narcissist, and a misogynist on top of it all. The sequences where we see him with his son Dean, whom he had with Carol, suggest there was at least a friendly relationship between the two. But the fact is that when young Dean Baker was seriously injured in a car accident, despite the repeated messages Carol left, Chet didn't even take the time to phone or write to see how the boy was faring.

And when Bruce Weber asks Baker's mother point blank whether she is disappointed by the way her son lived, Vera Baker responds, honestly and sadly, that she is.

When it comes to Chet Baker's relations with women, biographer James Gavin spares us no detail about the casual violence that characterized his behavior with them. Chet administered a dose of heroin to Sandy Jones, one of his girlfriends, against her will, then abandoned her in a coma-like state. Years later she recounted the time Chet tried to kill her, though she never understood why. He tied her arm and plunged in a needle. A couple of days later she came to. Baker had walked out, leaving her on the floor.

Weber's film doesn't focus on these incidents, though we do know that Baker, like his alcoholic father, had a habit of beating his women – sometimes in public. Carol was often spotted with a black eye. And it was common knowledge that Baker tried to strangle his lover Ruth Young with a phone cord. Another time he broke into her apartment to rob her and even sold her grand piano to pay for dope.

Of course, that doesn't take anything away from his musical talent. But Chet Baker was a vile human being, an absolute nihilist whose drug addiction would make writer William S. Burroughs or guitarist Keith Richards look like choirboys. A longtime colleague of his over the last years put it this way: "When you tour with Chet in Europe, the shortest trip between any two points always includes a stopover in Amsterdam."

"What's your favorite kind of high, Chet?" Bruce Weber asks the addicted jazzman in his film.

"Oh, the kind of high that scares other people to death. I guess they call it a speedball: it's a mixture of heroin and cocaine, you know."

In the documentary, as in real life, Chet is no more concerned with his own state than with those whose lives he helped ruin. As Hal Hinson pointed out in *The Washington Post* the day after the film premiered at the Toronto Film Festival, it is difficult, if not impossible to lift the human wreckage of little account that Chet Baker had become at the end of his career to the height of his own myth. All the film's dramatic tension flows from that difficulty, and Weber is fully aware of that.

~

A persistent rumor that I could never confirm, though it was mentioned in *Let's Get Lost*, is that Hollywood had wanted Chet for the lead role in the film *All the Fine Young Cannibals*. Reality check: the film was finished by the time he was arrested in Italy on June 30, 1960. According to what *The Hollywood Reporter* was saying as far back as April 1957, James Stewart and Lauren Bacall had, strangely enough, been slated for the lead roles. Whatever else came before, this mediocre melodrama ended up being directed by Michael Anderson and was very freely based on a comedy of manners called *The Bixby Girls* (1957) penned by Rosamond Marshall. Certain elements from Baker's life were added to the mix, and in the end the film starred Robert Wagner and Natalie Wood, on screen together for the first time. Our two lovebirds played Chad Bixby and Sarah "Salomé" Davis, a would-be modern-day Romeo and Juliet straight out of Pine Alley, a miserable crossroads somewhere in Texas.

The evening of the funeral for his father, the village pastor, Chad heads for the restaurant run by a sympathetic and maternal woman named Rose. The place is located in Deep Ellum, the Black section of town. He has come there to exorcize his grief by playing his trumpet, surrounded by his best friends, all Black, and the lovely Sarah whom he loves deeply. Both young people have problematic relations with their fathers. An only son, Chad will not forgive his deceased father for his intransigent racism that turned to violent punishment and left scars on the boy's body and soul forever. The eldest daughter of a family of eight, Sarah helps her mother raise her younger brothers and sisters but runs into conflict with her father about her habit of going out at night. The young couple's only refuge is their love, and we know from the start it is headed for tragedy. Then it happens. Sarah discovers she is pregnant with Chad's baby. He has neither money nor a future, so she decides to leave Pine Alley forever in search of better conditions for her unborn child.

On the train heading for the big city, she meets Tony McDowall, a rich man's son played by George Hamilton. Tony falls immediately in love with Sarah, who has taken on the name Salomé. Believing that the child on the way is his, he hurries to marry her and bring her into his stiff, upper-class world, much to the dismay of his sister Catherine (Susan Kohner) who considers the young woman unworthy of their clan. Meanwhile, thrown for a loop by his beloved's departure, Chad enters the circle of Rose's sister Ruby Jones, a blues and jazz singer and a sort of cinematic hybrid of Bessie Smith and Billie Holiday, played with a certain flair by Pearl Bailey who is unfortunately underutilized.

Their first exchange, in the wee hours, takes place at Rose's bar. Chad has come there after fighting his way out of a bad dream involving Sarah. Ruby offers her first bit of kindness: a drink. With her handkerchief, she dries the glass she was drinking from and pours Chad a generous shot of bourbon. He knocks it back in one gulp. Taking back the glass, Ruby wipes it again and serves herself an even more generous amount and drinks it down like water.

Trying to forget the man who broke her heart – it just so happens he was the trumpeter in her band – Ruby offers Chad a second kindness. She wants him to come home with her to New York so she can take care of him. "Let me do things for you, Chad," she begs him, trying to force him to wear her ex's coat. Stubbornly, he refuses, and though she is on shaky ground, she keeps pushing.

For reasons that are not exactly clear, the singer on her way down absolutely wants to help Chad launch a career in the music world. She goes as far as introducing him to her agent and insisting he find gigs for him playing trumpet. Inevitably, Tony and Salomé end up going to the chic club where Chad is playing. Bitter over the love of his life deserting him to raise his child with another man, Chad marries Catherine as an act of reprisal. This grade-B imitation of a Tennessee Williams play is a collection of unlikely turns of events and incongruous coincidences. With utter seriousness, the actors mouth the most awkward lines that fictional characters could ever speak.

In this comedy that is not meant to be one, only Pearl Bailey emerges unscathed. Robert Wagner does look almost convincing during the musical sequences, though his fingerings do not correspond to the notes that are supposed to be flowing from his trumpet. If we do accept the legend that the hero of *All the Fine Young Cannibals* was inspired by Chet Baker and that the part was meant for him, we have to wonder how the "James Dean of cool jazz" would have fit into the skin of Chad Bixby, his squeaky-clean alter ego. But that's a question that will never be answered…

Though they never offered him a role equal to his presumed talent as an actor, Hollywood remained obsessed with the figure of Chet Baker. There is no sense pouring over the very brief scene in *L.A. Confidential* (1997) directed by Curtis Hanson and based on a James Ellroy novel. The scene portrays Chet and Gerry Mulligan (that is, actors supposedly playing them) on the set of a TV production. Chet had at least one missed cinematic opportunity that we know about: the biopic that Dino De Laurentiis had planned to produce as the "Americano" was wasting away in a Roman jail cell – project called off. In the middle of the publicity campaign for *Born to Be Blue* (2015) in which he played the 40-year-old version of Chet, actor Ethan Hawke told the press that at one point, he had almost taken the part of a younger Chet Baker in a fiction film he had begun developing with director Richard Linklater in the middle of the 1990s, after they had watched *Let's Get Lost*, which had literally hypnotized both men.

Showing a fine sense of irony, director and screenwriter Robert Budreau set the action of *Born to Be Blue* at the end of the 1960s. In this "biographical fiction," this "reverie," we meet Chet Baker (Ethan Hawke) about to make a big-screen megaproduction based on his life of infamy and piloted by none other than… Dino De Laurentiis. Lady Luck is finally smiling on the jazzman, who is barely into his forties. Off the set, he has begun a romance with Jane, the actress who plays his lover Elaine. Then adversity strikes, as Chet is attacked after one of his concerts as a result of his unpaid drug debts.

With a broken jaw and his teeth knocked out, he's no use to the film anymore. He can't even play a single note. The production is put on the back burner indefinitely. Chet can count only on his own willpower and Jane's support to learn to play trumpet again and take back the spot he had with his peers, among them his friend Dizzy Gillespie (Kevin Hanchard), his rival Miles Davis (Kedar Brown), and his record producer Dick (Callum Keith Rennie).

For a first fiction film, Robert Budreau took on a real challenge. By choosing the 1960s, he placed his work at the very heart of a period of fundamental social and political turmoil around the question of race in the United States. He set out to portray a creator with his weaknesses and doubts, while trying to give a fair account of his contribution to music, his terrible addiction, and his downfall. Budreau seemed determined to avoid the usual stereotypes and traps of this kind of film. After all, like him, we all saw the worn-out narrative schemes of pictures like *Ray*, *Walk the Line*, and other biographical dramas. Budreau did a good job mixing reality and fiction. "Part of why I did this movie is that it's the anti-biopic," Ethan Hawke told Glenn Whipp of the *Los Angeles Times* in an interview published September 16, 2015, at the time *Born to Be Blue* premiered at the Toronto Film Festival. "It's fictional. It's imagining a moment in Chet's life. Did you read Geoff Dyer's book *But Beautiful?*"

Dyer, a British writer, presents a series of fictional portraits of seven legends of jazz: Charles Mingus, Duke Ellington, Thelonious Monk, Bud Powell, Chet Baker, Lester Young, and Art Pepper. Taking off from a true incident in their lives, a photo, or a simple anecdote, Dyer imagines impressionistic fantasies about crucial moments from which the music was born.

"That book is phenomenal," Hawke enthused in an interview. "So I read it, and this guy Robert Budreau read it. And he thought, 'What an idea. I'm going to take the legend of the person, the mythology and create a story about not as he was but how he could have been.' And the dream of the movie is that by liberating ourselves from nonfiction, we get at an essence of who he really was."

Fiction, biography, imaginary portraiture, reinvention of the facts. It doesn't matter what label you slap on those stories vaguely inspired by the lives of real people without the constraint of having to respect the little details. We have to accept them for what they are, with a grain of salt. Just as we need the same grain of salt to accept the representation of the relations between Chet Baker, Dizzy Gillespie, and Miles Davis put forward by *Born to Be Blue*. *Jazz Magazine* asked Gillespie to take the "blind test" during which an artist has to identify musicians who play the same instrument as him. Dizzy was not very charitable toward the young Chet Baker; he considered his sense of rhythm inadequate.

In *Miles* (1989), his autobiography written with journalist Quincy Troupe, Miles was indignant about the way white critics and audiences, from the moment he stepped on stage, classed Baker higher than Black trumpeters who were clearly superior to him when it came to technique and inspiration. All the critics were talking about Chet Baker when he was playing in Gerry Mulligan's band. He might as well have been the second coming of the Messiah, Miles rued. He accused Baker of sounding just like him. Self-doubt crept in. Miles found himself wondering if Baker could really play better than him and Dizzy and Clifford Brown.

A rancorous tone colors these comments, and with good reason. Long before white critics and audiences did the same, Charlie Parker, Miles' former mentor, had already anointed Chet after a tour together. Over the years, Baker attributed mythical status to his concerts with Bird, repeating what Parker said to his New York trumpet-playing friends about "a little white cat out here [in California] who's going to give you boys a lot of trouble." The reality is different. Pirated recordings from those fabled concerts at clubs like the Trade Winds and the Tiffany, which are now available ... on different labels, contradict Bird's supposed declarations and Baker's pretensions. His playing was still hesitant, his improvisations ragged, and the wave of notes flowing from Parker's and Sonny Criss' saxophones seemed to overwhelm him.

Unlike some of his colleagues and contemporaries, Dizzy Gillespie showed no resentment toward Chet Baker for his rapid critical and popular success that outstripped anything any other trumpeter knew at the beginning of the 1950s. For example, in July 1973, at the time of Chet's comeback that ended his seven-year absence from the stage, Dizzy spoke some encouraging words to the owners of the Half Note in Manhattan, which resulted in the ghost being offered a gig there for several weeks.

Miles is another story... According to James Gavin's book, one night ten years earlier, when Chet was playing at the Blue Note in New York, he spotted Miles in the house. At the break, he went over to his former mentor's table to greet him.

"Man, you suck!" Miles cackled in his gravelly voice, shaking his head in pity.

His pride wounded, Baker retreated into the wings and proceeded to shoot up.

It is no surprise that Baker, who was so enthralled by Miles' playing at the beginning, did not appreciate his stylistic evolution. The controlled freedom of his revolutionary second quintet in the 1960s and his flirtation with rock that followed left Baker cold. "Those aren't even melodies," he complained to a French jazz magazine. He understood nothing of his former idol's music and certainly had no desire to try and play it.

At that point in his career, Chet considered himself a victim of reverse discrimination. Music critics did not take him seriously anymore, and record producers and nightclub owners would not offer him contracts because he was white.

∽

When we watch and hear Baker singing in *Let's Get Lost*, he gives off a kind of emotion that solicits our sympathy. We can't help feeling it because we know that this truly is his swan song.

On May 13, 1988, in Laren, not far from Amsterdam, Chet was to share the stage with sax player Archie Shepp for a concert that would be broadcast live on European radio. Strange bedfellows, it's true, this match between one of the fiery champions of free jazz and the incarnation of the cool style who hadn't changed his tune in 30 years. Two hours before the concert, the promoter passed by the hotel to pick Baker up and learned that he had never checked in. A search party was organized, but he was nowhere to be found, not even in his usual spots.

Always in need of money for dope, Baker was not one to miss a concert. In the spring of 1988, his daily consumption of heroin stood at six grams. He shot it into his scrotum, since he could not find a vein anywhere else in his body. To maintain his high, he would sniff one line of coke after another between shooting up. When his Alfa Romeo approached the concert hall with his dealer Bob Holland at the wheel, Chet was still missing. Holland had not seen him since he had gone looking for more medicine for him, two days earlier. Chet was very upset by the fight he had with his lover Diane Vavra, who had left him after he raised his hand against her one time too many. "I'm 58 years old, Bob," Baker reportedly said as he stuck the needle in. "I've used this stuff for 30 years. You can't help me. I'm too far out."

In the wee hours, the Amsterdam police came upon the body of a man in the fetal position on the sidewalk in front of a cheap hotel, his face bloodied, his skull fractured. The police surmised the man had thrown himself from a window of the Prins Hendrik Hotel and that the skull fracture was due to the impact when he hit the concrete below. The man had no papers on him. His body was wrapped in a white sheet and sent to the morgue.

The next morning, the detectives who returned to the Prins Hendrik determined that the room overlooking the spot where they discovered the unidentified body had been rented by a certain Chet Baker. The name meant nothing to them. The room was locked from the inside. The keys were still there, along with two glasses: one with a syringe containing a gram of heroin and the other with a mixture of heroin and coke. They also found a trumpet in the room, along with a bracelet, a lighter, and a few coins stuffed in a bag. Before they received the autopsy report that revealed dope in the dead man's veins, the police figured it was just another suicidal junkie. But the little window was not open wide enough for a man, even one as slender as Baker, to slip through it for the fatal fall.

Over the next quarter century, the circumstances of Chet Baker's death generated a good number of questions and just as many legends. Did he succumb to an overdose? Was he pushed by a dealer to whom he owed money? Did he simply kill himself? Tom Schnabel, the famous host and producer of jazz shows for KCRW, a California public radio station, told an enlightening story on his *Rhythm Planet* blog.

One evening, during a radio interview with James Gavin about his Baker biography, after Schnabel discussed the artistic uncertainty that surrounded the musician's final moments in this vale of tears, he received a phone call from a listener who said he was in Amsterdam the night Baker died. He happened to be staying at the same hotel and claimed to have seen and heard Chet chatting with a woman in the lobby. Apparently, the jazzman went up to his room to fetch his cigarettes and realized he had forgotten his keys inside. The door to the next room was open, so he went in, then out onto the balcony. As he was trying to make it over to the balcony of his room, he lost his balance and fell to his death. Then the man who called Schnabel ended this way: "Ask Little Jimmy Scott. He was there at the hotel and he remembers."

A few months later, Schnabel went to hear Little Jimmy Scott, a jazz singer with an eternally androgynous, prepubescent voice and "perhaps the most unjustly ignored American singer of the 20th century," according to the *New York Times*. After the performance, Schnabel questioned Scott about Amsterdam. Yes, he had been there, Scott confirmed, on the night of Chet Baker's accidental death. He corroborated what the listener had said down to the smallest detail.

No doubt the emotion that takes hold of us as we listen to Chet sing in *Let's Get Lost* owes something to the fact that we know the musician is literally at the end of his rope. To echo critic Hal Hinson from the *Washington Post*, sometimes Baker made us feel he was detached from his own performances, as if he were singing about a dream of love, though he had only a vague recollection of it, and had stopped believing in it a long time ago.

In that sense, his rendition of Elvis Costello's "Almost Blue" is perfect, since the song is about almost feeling something.

"There's a girl here and she's almost you," the lyrics go. We're free to interpret what Costello's devastating line meant to Chet Baker.

With a speedball keeping him going, the fallen angel of cool jazz really does appear disincarnate in the film, especially in the sequences when he speaks directly to the camera. Toward the end of *Let's Get Lost*, when Bruce Weber, off screen, asks Chet if he enjoyed the experience of being filmed, he answers coolly, "How the hell could I've seen it? [...] It was like in a dream."

Almost.

Spike Lee

Jazz, Masculinity, and the
Persistence of the Blues

T he night is no longer young in a Harlem whipped by torrential rains and bathed in indigo light. A man's face silhouetted in the bluish light across from the Dizzy Club. Felt hat, pale raincoat, trumpet case over one shoulder. He reads the marquee. THE SHADOW HENDERSON QUARTET, FEATURING CLARKE BETANCOURT.

The man marches across the street and heads straight for the doorman, a dwarf ironically nicknamed Giant. Giant can't believe his eyes. Bleek, Bleek Gilliam! The two childhood friends haven't seen each other since the gruesome incident in the back alley that changed their lives. Spotting the trumpet case, Giant, who was once Bleek's manager, asks if he'll be sitting in with the band. If and only if Shadow gives permission, Bleek replies. Giant turns and escorts his friend inside for his return performance.

On stage, in a sheath of a dress that leaves little to the imagination, Clarke Betancourt launches into the first verse with minimal accompaniment:

You can never tell what's in a man's mind
And if he is from Harlem, there's no use of even tryin'
Just like the tide, his mind comes and goes
Like March weather, when he'll change
Nobody knows, nobody knows.

The lament about the inconsistency of men flows through the crowded club and seems headed straight for Bleek. Not so long ago, Clarke was his girl, not Shadow's. She was one of his two lovers, and he refused to choose between them, preferring his music most of all.

He stands frozen to the spot, letting the song envelope him. Back when they were together, she often asked him to listen to her demo tape and let her sit in with him on stage. He never, ever paid even a second of attention to the recording. And suddenly, she sings magnificently, her voice an instrument perfectly mastered.

For him, it's an epiphany.

While Shadow weaves a poignant counterpoint around the verses and refrains, Clarke wraps up her interpretation of "Harlem Blues," sending Bleek a tender smile, free of resentment. The song lyrics seem to have been written for just this occasion, though they are usually attributed to W. C. Handy, who may have penned them in 1922, with the help of elements lifted from traditional songs from the public domain. The words might be immemorial, but Bleek knows Clarke has made them speak for the two of them, for what was and will never be again.

The crowd breaks into a wave of warm applause. "Clarke sure can sing!" Giant shouts to Bleek through the noise, though the latter needs no outside confirmation. Clarke steps away from the mike to let Shadow announce the arrival of a great musician who is also a dear friend and invites him on stage: "Please give a warm welcome to Mr. Bleek Gilliam! Bleek!" Applause breaks out for a second time as the trumpeter makes his way forward, feeling like an ex-boxer wondering whether he should have stepped back into the ring. He puts his arms around Shadow for a moment, and then Clarke and the other musicians from what was once his quintet. He brings his trumpet to his lips and begins to explore the theme of one of his own compositions,with a title that says it all: "Again, Never."

After a few measures, the unthinkable happens. As his ex-lover and her new man look on in disbelief, the virtuoso trumpeter, who spent his childhood practicing under his mother's supervision instead of running in the park with his pals, plays one sour note after another. He's out of tune; the melody disintegrates. Bleek's lips, turned into pulp by thugs one night in the alley, are not up to the job anymore. He has lost control of his instrument. He panics and breaks off the piece. From the rear of the stage, Shadow hesitates but has no choice. He lifts his soprano sax to his mouth and tries to save the situation by taking up the lyricism of the theme that the trumpeter he invited on stage has massacred.

As Clarke looks on sadly, Bleek leaves her side and moves through the club as fast as he can, heading for the exit. He is a wreck, in utter distress. The rain pours down on the Harlem streets. Under the club's marquee, he hands the trumpet to his friend Giant. He can't use it anymore.

Giant has followed him outside, offering futile words of comfort. Forgetting that he hasn't put his raincoat back on, Bleek goes out into the indigo night, looking for salvation elsewhere.

~

This emotional scene that you may recall is drawn from one of my favorite Spike Lee films, *Mo' Better Blues* (1990). Denzel Washington stars in the role of the egocentric Bleek Gilliam, Wesley Snipes plays his friend and rival Shadow Henderson, and Cynda Williams is the sensual Clarke. Lee himself takes the role of Giant, whose addiction to gambling and whose debts will cost the trumpeter dearly.

There have been a number of films recently set in and around the world of jazz: *Whiplash* (2014) and *La La Land* (2016) by Damien Chazelle, Robert Budreau's *Born to Be Blue* (2015) that we have explored, and *Miles Ahead* by and with Don Cheadle (2016). Some time ago, I had the pleasure of watching this work from Spike Lee's youth – he was hardly 30 years old when he directed it. In April 2009, we met in a Montreal bistro during the retrospective of his works that the Cinémathèque Québécoise had organized. He was surprised and intrigued that I was so enthusiastic about that film. "What do you like about it so much?" he wanted to know. "The music, mostly," I answered straight off.

The soundtrack album that issued from *Mo' Better Blues* has a special place in my personal collection. It is quite short, though it does include the seven major pieces played on screen by the protagonists, with two separate versions of "Harlem Blues." There is an acid jazz track by Gang Starr & Dream Warriors, shot through with spoken and musical samplings celebrating the history and the heroes of jazz ("Jazz Thing"). Is that cut a concession to current trends, or the illustration of the relation between jazz and hip hop? There's no telling. Except for that track that runs during the final credits and the unforgettable principal theme composed by Bill Lee, a bassist, composer, and the father of the director, all the pieces bear the signature of Branford Marsalis. He was already well known by that time, notably for his 1980s contribution to the emergence of neo-bop led by his younger trumpeter brother Wynton. Branford's fame increased thanks to his work with Sting after The Police broke up. He played on Sting albums such as *The Dream of the Blue Turtles* (1985), *Bring on the Night* (1986), and *Nothing Like the Sun* (1987), all on the A&M label.

Thanks to a strong media presence, he appears in the film, as does Jeff "Tain" Watts, who steps in as drummer Rhythm Jones. Marsalis' quartet, with the addition of Terence Blanchard, a New Orleans trumpeter and Branford's old friend, recorded the music for Bleek's quintet and Shadow Henderson. Marsalis and Blanchard also coached Wesley Snipes and Denzel Washington so they would look as though they were really playing their instruments.

Spike Lee's films take on what's essential in today's America: racial tensions, class differences, battles between the sexes, the difficulty people have escaping the predefined frameworks of social norms. Very often, the main characters are caught between the need to belong to their group and the desire to express themselves freely. *Mo' Better*

Blues fits right in with that pattern. The film presents the fictional alter ego of a Wynton Marsalis or a Wallace Roney, respectively considered as a purist attached to an idealized orthodox tradition and a progressive visionary of jazz. Still, nuance is necessary. In a conversation, Roney told me, "I remember, Spike Lee used to come and listen to me and my group when he was writing his script." But outside of a few visual elements involving posture and attitude, he did not see anything that Lee might have borrowed from him to invent his Bleek Gilliam character.

Bleek has a studious quality and a desire to innovate, which is paradoxically twinned with a fidelity to jazz tradition, seen as the absolute expression of African American culture. These paradoxes lead to conflicts with the members of his group, especially saxophonist Shadow Henderson. The two men's friendship includes both a sense of brotherhood and masculine rivalry that is not always very healthy.

In his article "Signifying the Phallus: *Mo' Better Blues* and Representations of the Jazz Trumpet" (*Cinema Journal*, vol. 32, no. 1, autumn 1992), Krin Gabbard (today, in retirement, an adjunct professor at Columbia University) postulates that, as far back as the days of Louis Armstrong, the jazz trumpet symbolized a certain idea of Black masculinity with a freight of sexual connotations. Pursuing his *idée fixe*, Gabbard points out that the bell of Dizzy Gillespie's trumpet, aiming upward, helped the father of bebop hear himself better on a crowded, noisy stage, but also (and most of all) asserted the phallic aspect and character of the premier jazz instrument. According to Gabbard, the tonality, rapidity, and intensity of emotion, and even the posture of trumpet players like Satchmo and Dizzy, exuded a powerful "libidinal force."

There is an exception to this stereotype of Black priapism, and Gabbard accepts it. He discusses women trumpeters, a rare breed in the days of swing and be-bop. But he commits the error of citing the little-known Rebecca Coupe Franks, a contemporary artist, and white as well, whereas Maxine Sullivan would have been a better example for him. Trumpet and trombone player, singer and orchestra leader who made her debut in the 1930s, Satchmo's screen partner in the film *Going Places* (1938), Sullivan stands as a counterweight to the exuberant Black virility of the Armstrong/Gillespie school. Yet Gabbard identifies Miles Davis as the one who changed the tune with his cool, "post-phallic" approach. At the end of the 1940s, he developed an explicitly introspective style, both contemplative and lyrical. As a young man, Miles had a fragile image; he played as if he were walking on eggs.

Krin Gabbard puts Terence Blanchard in the same category. Not surprising, since Davis sang his praises from the very moment he joined a late version of Art Blakey's Jazz Messengers. Gabbard, an academic, contested the choice of Blanchard as Denzel Washington's coach. According to him, Blanchard was less able to communicate Bleek Gilliam's male chauvinism than a more "virile" musician like Jon Faddis, Dizzy's heir apparent. Yet the film brims over with Bleek's macho. There's the sequence where he runs his horn over Clarke's body as a way of urging her to undress, and he refuses to choose between her and his other lover Indigo. "It's a dick thing," says the stickman to justify his modus operandi.

Despite the reductive idea Gabbard defends in his article, Terence Blanchard's playing goes far beyond the fragile tone associated with the young Miles Davis in his cool period. We only have to look at his work on *Mo' Better Blues*, his albums with the Jazz Messengers, the group he co-led with saxophonist Donald Harrison, and subsequent bands he piloted by himself. On certain cuts of the soundtrack (for example, "Say Hey" and the hit parade parody, "Pop Top 40," laid down by Bleek), Blanchard machineguns notes at an all-out rate. Virile but soaring, he takes on the upper register of his instrument. The echoes of the marching bands of his native New Orleans are there in his phrasing that conjures up Armstrong's hot style more than Davis' cool themes. On "Knocked out the Box," the piece that accompanies the extremely violent scene in the alley where Giant gets beaten up by his bookie's thugs for unpaid debts, just behind the Beneath the Underdog club where Bleek is holding court, Blanchard moves very close to the excesses of free jazz.

It's hard to know if Spike Lee deliberately decided to attenuate the image of the Black trumpeter as champion male chauvinist, the way Krin Gabbard suggests. Maybe the filmmaker was not trying to shore up that hypothetical link between the hot trumpet style and runaway virility. The blues and the inner pain that fills Bleek Gilliam can be expressed in a introspective style. To Gabbard's credit, he is right to remind us that Hollywood has been struggling for three-quarters of a century with just this kind of representation. Louis Armstrong inevitably ended up with roles as the sexless court jester or the comical, inoffensive yes-man. The emasculation of the jazz trumpeter, according to Gabbard, wipes away considerations of race. He draws a parallel between the white character of Rick Martin played by Kirk Douglas in *Young Man with a Horn* (1950) and that of Bleek Gilliam. Martin's inability to navigate the higher notes of the register during a recording session with singer Jo Jordan (Doris Day) can be seen as a metaphor for his artistic impotence. Bleek's breakdown on stage at the Dizzy Club next to Clarke and the man who replaced him in his ex-lover's bed serves as an echo of that scene.

Mo' Better Blues does offer its hero a way out. After he is struck by sudden and definitive musical impotence, Bleek gives up on the art. His next move is to beg Indigo, his other ex-lover, to save him by marrying him and becoming the mother of his children. Whereas his own mother forced him to learn music to the detriment of a normal boy's life, Bleek, a father now, will break the cycle by letting his son set his trumpet on the shelf and head out to the streets of Brooklyn to play with his friends. All's well that ends well, for once.

∾

To settle the question, if it can be settled, I will look to the similarity between that key film scene at the Dizzy Club, and this story told, then contested by Miles Davis in his autobiography. By the way, his book appears on screen, in Bleek's library.

According to the legend, in 1954, one rainy night, Clifford Brown, the fiery hard-bop trumpeter and successor to Dizzy Gillespie and Fats Navarro, was playing Detroit with his quintet. Miles showed up at the venue, completely stoned, soaked to the skin, his horn wrapped in brown paper. The legend says that he stumbled on stage without being invited up and awkwardly tried to play "My Funny Valentine," though he was incapable of squeezing out the melody of this well-known standard. Clifford Brown had to step in and save him from himself – and he was completely up to the job.

Humiliated by his younger colleague, Miles left the stage without asking for a second chance. He went back out into the rain from which he'd come.

The man himself maintained that no such event ever took place. It was in his interest to deny it. Though he insisted the legend was invented, he did recognize that it would have made a great scene in a movie.

Spike Lee, who directed *Mo' Better Blues*, obviously agreed. The lonely musician who disappears into the indigo of a rainy night is one of the archetypes of the blues, and jazz owes much to it.

Miles Davis

On Screen, On Canvas

Tutu, a film released in September 1986 and awarded two Grammys (Best Jazz Instrumental Performance, Soloist and Best Album of the Year – Jazz), represents a turning point in Miles Davis' art. It was his first record with Warner after 30 years with Columbia. His defection stemmed from his resentment. The latter company, so he believed, was paying more attention to Wynton Marsalis than to him.

From the point of view of esthetics, *Tutu* is one of the major works in Miles' discography. The record is more revolutionary than evolutionary. Up until then, the stylistic changes that marked his career were progressive, the results of discoveries and intuitions already present in his work. The music of his cool jazz nonet was based on the harmonies of be-bop. His big band with Gil Evans on *Miles Ahead*, *Porgy and Bess*, and *Sketches of Spain* were extrapolations taken from what the nonet had offered. The modal improvisations of *Kind of Blue* had their antecedents in *Milestones* and *Porgy and Bess*. The crossover into rock on *Bitches Brew* had been underway since *Miles in the Sky*, *Filles de Kilimanjaro*, and *In a Silent Way* – and so it went.

As much by its sound as by the new technologies that made it possible, *Tutu* is a radical departure from all that went before. Instead of interacting in real time with a group of musicians, Miles essentially improvised over electronic audio canvases set up ahead of time by multi-instrumentalist, composer, and arranger Marcus Miller, to whom he entrusted the album's concept. Of course, on previous records, Davis and his producers used editing, collage, and over-dubbing on multiple tracks, methods usually used in pop. On *Sketches of Spain*, for instance, certain orchestral passages were recorded without Miles; his solos were added afterward. But this was the first time his trumpet was laid over an almost entirely synthetic surface, except for the playing of a number of soloists invited into the project. There was George Duke on keyboards, the Polish violinist Michal Urbaniak, synthesizer programmer Jason Miles, and, from time to time, Marcus Miller on bass clarinet. Now and again, vocal samplings – like Miles' background grumbling or the famous "One mo' time" from Count Basie tunes – add additional color to the canvas.

These innovations quickly set off a controversy. The purists wondered: is it still jazz if the soloist is not engaged in improvised dialogue with other musicians?

The album's title carries a double meaning. It's a tip of the hat to South Africa's Archbishop Desmond Tutu, winner of the 1984 Nobel Peace Prize and leader of the anti-apartheid movement. And in the Yoruba language of southwest Nigeria, the word means "cool" and refers to the idea of grace under pressure. That description couldn't be more appropriate for Miles Davis. Warner decided to go whole hog when it came to promoting the album. The label turned to Spike Lee, whose career was skyrocketing, and asked him to direct a video for MTV. It was among the specialized networks that broadcasted short films to teenage audiences, and the majors wanted to sell records to them.

Lee was the right choice. He had won, one after the other, the Prix de la Jeunesse from the Cannes Film Festival, the Los Angeles Film Critics Association's New Generation Award, and the Independent Spirit Award for Best First Feature for *She's Gotta Have It*. The film is a black-and-white comedy of manners about a sexually insatiable young woman and her three lovers. Between this film and his next, Spike Lee made his first music video, "Royal Garden Blues" based on a standard by Clarence and Spencer Williams and revisited by saxophonist Branford Marsalis' group. Marsalis, too, was an emerging star and would work with Lee again a few years later on *Mo' Better Blues*.

The images of his "Tutu Medley" move to the sound of excerpts from the record. There's the cover track, followed by "Tomaas," "Portia," and "Splatch." Sequences show Miles in a variety of flamboyant outfits, improvising as he travels down a corridor or paces through a minimally decorated loft. Then Lee has Miles painting female forms and other colorful shapes in art naïf fashion with African influences.

The association between Miles and visual media certainly did not begin with this video. Very early in his career, critics and commentators wore out their metaphors describing his playing as pointillist and elliptical. In the liner notes for *Kind of Blue*, pianist Bill Evans makes the connection between his band leader's music and a form of Japanese art that depends on spontaneity, in which the artist must paint on thin stretched parchment with a special brush. Any interrupted stroke will break through the parchment, and erasures are impossible. The resulting compositions might lack complexity, but they capture a kind of spontaneity.

Obviously, Miles Davis is not the first jazz musician (or musician of any kind for that matter) to have picked up a brush, nor the first to have had their music compared to the works of the great painters. As a child, Duke Ellington learned painting along with piano. When it comes to Miles, the recurrent analogy between his music and the visual arts is more accurate than the image of "the man walking on eggs" that was long used to describe his playing. The man's interest in visual art began early in the 1980s. Miles spoke eloquently about this subject to Quincy Troupe, who co-authored Davis' autobiography. He began to draw on a European tour. It was a form of therapy, he admitted, something to do with his spare time now that he wasn't smoking or drinking or snorting. It sprang from the need to keep himself occupied so he wouldn't start thinking about doing those kinds of things.

Far be it from me seeing in Davis a second Robert Ryman, though his is an intriguing story. A young music-lover leaves Nashville for New York in 1952 in hopes of making a career for himself as a sax player, and ends up as one of the most influential American painters of the second half of the twentieth century. Vittorio Colaizzi, an art history professor at Old Dominion University in Norfolk, Virginia wrote a monograph about Ryman that is worth a look. But unlike him, Davis never abandoned music for painting. And despite the pecuniary value they acquired, mainly because of the jazzman's fame, his paintings never had the same impact as his music and certainly never influenced anyone the way Ryman's abstract works did.

Miles was often compared to Picasso, since they both kept moving forward in new ways, turning away from past successes to try something more exciting. The comparison eventually became a cliché. Outmoded or not, there is a genuine parallel between the creators of *Kind of Blue* and *Guernica*. Very few artists influenced their disciplines the way those two legends did. And they weren't afraid to disappoint their fans' expectations when they needed to in order to create something that had never been seen or heard before.

∿

During every stage of his career, Miles Davis showed a real interest in visual media. In 1957, after being the revelation of the Newport Jazz Festival the year before, ushered in the front door at Columbia Records, his star was on the rise. Then fate smiled further: through a happy set of circumstances, he was offered the soundtrack for the first film by a young French director whom Juliette Gréco introduced him to; at the time, she and Miles were lovers. The beginner's name was Louis Malle. Very much under the influence of Hitchcock, this French film noir, adapted from the Noël Calef novel that came out the year before, *Ascenseur pour l'échafaud*, or *Elevator to the Gallows*, would be one of the keystones of the New Wave movement in France and elsewhere.

The plot is both simple and twisted, and pure Hitchcock. One Friday before leaving work, Tavernier, a former paratrooper in France's colonial wars, commits the perfect crime: he kills his boss Carala in cold blood with the help of the victim's wife, Florence. Of course, the two are lovers. He wants to eliminate a compromising clue left on the scene of the murder-disguised-as-suicide, and in the process, he gets stuck in an elevator. Florence waits for him in vain in a café, then spends the night wandering in the rain in search of him. Meanwhile, a young deliveryman steals Tavernier's car to impress his girlfriend. During their joyride, the man, panicking, uses Tavernier's gun to kill two German tourists staying at the same hotel as him and his girlfriend. All the while, Tavernier does everything in his power to escape the elevator car stuck between two floors.

On the night of December 4, 1957, in the Poste Parisien studio, with a group of expatriate American and French musicians accompanying him on a brief European tour, Miles recorded the soundtrack's themes, and so brought modern jazz into French cinema.

A fascinating news clip from French television about that session opens with a close up of Davis improvising over blues chords, his eyes on the film's black-and-white images. Then the scene moves to the control room, where François Chalais, a journalist from the French network RTF, is interviewing the director.

> CHALAIS: What exactly is happening?
> MALLE: The American musician Miles Davis is improvising to scenes from my film *Elevator to the Gallows*.
> CHALAIS: Do you mean he's looking at the images and playing trumpet to what he sees?
> MALLE: Yes. These are images he knows very well, since he has seen the film. And we have talked about what we might do, and then, with his group, we screen the film and he records.
> CHALAIS: He didn't write out a partition ahead of time?
> MALLE: Absolutely not.
> CHALAIS: It just comes to him?
> MALLE: It just comes to him.
> CHALAIS: If he had come tomorrow, it would have been different music?
> MALLE: Yes. And from one take to the next, it changes.

Okay, there is no partition, but indications, precise at times, laconic in other places, were given to his bandmates during the session. The method used for that evening's work prefigures the creation of his absolute masterpiece, *Kind of Blue*, over two afternoons (March 2 and April 22, 1959). That time, he simply handed a series of scales to the musicians of his sextet; they were to improvise each piece from them.

In his preface to this masterwork, pianist Bill Evans

goes back to his parchment metaphor: just as a painter needs a framework of parchment, a musical group, to improvise, needs a framework in time. Davis' frameworks were exquisite in their simplicity, yet contained everything necessary to stimulate spontaneous performance.

We could say the same for the music of *Elevator to the Gallows*. In a number of ways, it is a kind of prototype for *Kind of Blue*.

I wouldn't go so far as to claim that Louis Malle started a trend when he asked Davis to create his film's soundtrack. Yet other French directors from the time immediately followed suit. As mentioned, Édouard Molinaro recruited Art Blakey and his Jazz Messengers for *The Road to Shame* (1959). Not to be outdone, and taking second helpings, Roger Vadim retained not only Blakey's services, but those of Duke Jordan and Thelonious Monk for *Les Liaisons dangereuses 1960* (1959). Meanwhile, Jean-Luc Godard turned to a rising star of French jazz, Martial Solal, for the music for *Breathless* (*À bout de souffle*) from 1960. For his famous *Paris Blues* from 1961, which very much looks like a pastiche of French New Wave films, American Martin Ritt hired Louis Armstrong and Duke Ellington. The latter had authored the music for Otto Preminger's *Anatomy of a Murder* (1959).

Though Miles did admit to enjoying the experience with *Elevator to the Gallows* – he called it "formative" in his autobiography – he did not go back to the film for another dozen years. In 1970, as a musician, but also a boxing fan and amateur boxer himself, he was asked to compose the music for Bill Clayton's documentary about Jack Johnson, the "Galveston Giant," the first African American to hold the title of heavyweight world champion from 1908 to 1915. As the century progressed, he became an emblem of Black pride. And with reason: in 1913, he was imprisoned for having a relationship with a white woman. In a move that astonished everyone, in 2018 Donald Trump posthumously pardoned him. When it came to Ken Burns' turn to devote a documentary to the boxer (*Unforgivable Blackness: The Rise and Fall of Jack Johnson*), he would ask Wynton Marsalis to provide the soundtrack. I think I see a trend developing…

Inspired by the boxer and the strong identification he had with him, Miles delivered two long tracks to Clayton. Each occupied one side of the LP *A Tribute to Jack Johnson* that came out in 1971: "Right Off" and "Yesternow." Beginning in 1966, the studio had been a place of ongoing experimentation for Miles. The mikes were on all the time and the tape was always rolling. Everything that happened there up until 1975 was systematically recorded and stored in the Columbia vaults. Teo Macero, Miles' producer, was responsible for sorting and cutting and editing, in theory according to the trumpeter's directions. On *A Tribute to Jack Johnson*, Macero used the results of two sessions set down on April 7, 1970, as well as some outtakes from the 1969 sessions that had produced *In a Silent Way*, and even an unpublished fragment that arose from a recording with Gil Evans. It served as the soundtrack for the conclusion orated in grand style by actor Brock Peters, who played the boxer: *I'm Jack Johnson, heavyweight champion of the world. I'm Black. They never let me forget it. I'm Black all right! I'll never let them forget it!*

This challenge issued by Johnson via Peters would not

be out of place coming from Miles Davis. He deplored the fact that his record label was so reticent about promoting a work so important to him. When the album came out, he remarked bitterly, the label buried it. One of the reasons, he believed, was because it was music you could dance to. It had a lot in common with what white rock musicians were playing, and the company didn't want a Black jazz musician doing that kind of music. So Columbia didn't promote it.

~

"Painting helps me with my music," the trumpeter says in his autobiography. Between January 31 and February 4, 1985, he took part in a project that brought together his two artistic passions. That was the recording of the "Aura" suite, composed in his honor by Danish trumpet player Palle Mikkelborg, after Miles was awarded the Léonie Sonning Music Prize in December 1984. A mixed bag of classical impressionism, new European music, jazz, rock, reggae, electronic, and other musical genres, the suite opens with the main theme made of the ten notes corresponding to the letters of Miles Davis' name, over a sustained chord of the same notes. The nine movements that follow represent the colors that Mikkelborg attributed to Miles' aura, from "White" to "Violet" with a stop at "Electric Red."

Miles was in no small measure proud to have received the prize usually reserved for prestigious composers and classical musicians. Proud also to have recorded the album with some of the greatest names in jazz like Danish bassist

Niels-Henning Ørsted Pedersen and a former colleague, British guitarist John McLaughlin. The first Miles recording with an orchestra in over 20 years, *Aura* was not a conventional big band album. Quite far from Duke Ellington-style swing, this atypical work is like jazz fusion with modern classical accents. Many passages speak of the influence that composers Olivier Messiaen and Charles Ives had on Mikkelborg.

Because of the contract dispute based on Miles' "defection" to Warner, Columbia Records would not issue the album until September 1989, making *Aura* one of the last original records to be released before he died. Miles called it a true masterpiece, and would earn two more Grammys thanks to it: Best Jazz Instrumental Performance, Soloist; and Best Jazz Instrumental Performance, Big Band.

Since the early 1980s, Davis had learned to love the greater media attention he was receiving. He began showing up unexpectedly on the screen, and here I am not referring to late-night talk shows or concert recordings from around the world. He appeared on TV ads for Honda scooters as part of a series starring popular music celebrities like Lou Reed, Adam Ant, Grace Jones, and the group Devo. "Those commercials got me more recognition than anything else I have ever done," he said.

In the fall of 1985, he joined an episode in the second season of *Miami Vice*, the late, lamented cop show. "Junk Love," it was called, and he played a pimp named Ivory Jones. He had this to say about his modest beginnings as an actor in his autobiography:

Acting wasn't that hard. I knew how to play a pimp because I knew a little bit about that from the old days. Don Johnson and Philip Michael Thomas, the actors on the show, just told me, "Man, it's nothing, nothing but lies. Miles. Nothing but lies. So just think of it that way," and I did.

When he was asked how he saw the actor's job, he answered, "You're acting all the time when you're Black. Black people are acting out roles every day in this country just to keep on getting by." He did admit he was not too happy to be playing a pimp and reinforcing the stereotyped vision of Black people on television. He preferred to see himself as a kind of businessman.

A year later, he accepted an offer from director Mary Lambert and her producers and put together the soundtrack for a feature-length fiction film, *Siesta*. Very much in the shadow of *Tutu* that had come out the previous year, the music for this fantasy drama, with its stylized look that pastiches *The Twilight Zone*, is esthetically closer to the 1960 *Sketches of Spain* that he recorded with Gil Evans' orchestra. And there was a reason for that.

Both psychological thriller and surrealistic fantasy, *Siesta* boasted an entire battalion of stars: Ellen Barkin, Gabriel Byrne, Julian Sands, Jodie Foster, Martin Sheen, Isabella Rossellini, and Grace Jones. Set mainly in Madrid, it is Mary Lambert's first film; before it, she was one of the most sought-after music video directors around. She had worked with Annie Lennox, Sting, Mick Jagger, as well as Madonna on celebrated clips like "Borderline," "Like a

Virgin," "Material Girl," "La Isla Bonita," and "Like a Prayer." Shortly before, she was on Prince's team for his film *Under the Cherry Moon* (1986) but was fired by His Purple Majesty after a few weeks of shooting.

While she was editing *Siesta*, as a guide track Lambert used *Sketches of Spain*, one of her favorite albums, though it did not occur to her to hire Miles Davis to write an original soundtrack. The production opted for a Tom Tom Club song, and another from the tandem of Wendy & Lisa, musicians very close to Prince, which proved that Lambert did not bear a grudge. But those excerpts didn't seem to work with the film, and Lambert kept returning to *Sketches*. One of her producers, Gary Kurfirst, suggested she solicit Miles Davis' help. To do so, she went through Tommy LiPuma at Warner Records.

We can hear Lambert's memories of that first meeting in an interview she gave the "thelastmiles.com" site. She was warned that Davis would be hostile and surly. She had been directing videos, though so she was used to handling divas. Miles showed up in the biggest Ferrari with the biggest engine. He got out of the car and they just got along right away. She said "Hi, Miles," and he said "Hi, Mary." They watched the movie and he was really attentive.

Miles turned to his new right-hand man, Marcus Miller, who now played the role Gil Evans once did when it came to his projects. He gave laconic instructions to Miller: "Write some music and it should sound something like this. And when you need a trumpet, just let me know." Miles had obviously taken to the way of working he had used for *Tutu*, and it became his modus operandi for the rest of his life.

Mary Lambert got what she wanted. The *Siesta* soundtrack evoked an Iberian-tinged melancholy that echoed *Sketches of Spain*, but with one major difference. The high-flying lyricism of Gil Evans' orchestra was replaced by Miller's sequencers and synthesizers, though he did take the trouble to integrate flamenco guitar solos by Earl Klugh, metallic sounds, sighs, and his own work on bass and clarinet. Topping off this exotic wash were the striking lamentations of Miles' trumpet, like the last light of dying day before the shadows take over for good.

Labeled "this year's *Blue Velvet*" by *American Film*, *Siesta* earned its director a nomination for the Independent Spirit Awards for Best First Feature Film. But it very quickly fell into limbo land and is now remembered only for its soundtrack.

A year after *Siesta* came *Street Smart* (1987), directed by Jerry Schatzberg with Christopher Reeve in the role of a journalist investigating the world of prostitution. It, too, was quickly forgotten despite the soundtrack co-composed by Davis and his keyboard player Robert Irving III. This time, Warner didn't bother making a record of it, which may have been a disavowal of the music Miles said he was so proud of. Regardless, we are a long way from *Elevator to the Gallows*.

The year 1988 saw the release of *Scrooged*. It was a mediocre adaptation-update of Charles Dickens' *A Christmas Carol* directed by Richard Donner, with Bill Murray in the lead role. The movie did allow Miles-watchers a quick glimpse of him on the big screen. As Murray's character and his friends push their way down a crowded street, we can see a small sign reading "Feed the Starving Musicians." The musicians in question are part of a combo featuring Miles on trumpet and David Sanborn on alto sax playing a funky arrangement of "We Three Kings of Orient Are." Murray, the head of a TV network in the picture, a cynical, selfish careerist, tosses a few coins into their instrument case and comments, "Rip off the hicks, why don't you? Did you learn the song yesterday?"

The next big-screen project Miles got involved with gave him the opportunity to musically converse with a giant of the blues, John Lee Hooker. Opening at the 1990 Toronto International Film Festival, *The Hot Spot* is based on a 1953 novel by Charles Williams, *Hell Hath No Fury*. Williams wrote the screenplay himself, hoping it would attract Robert Mitchum. The work lay dormant for almost 40 years until the day Dennis Hopper stumbled upon it. The actor and director had known Miles since the end of his teenage years. Hopper told a story that had Davis beating up a pusher who was about to sell heroin to him, then swearing to Hopper that he'd kill him if he ever found out he used.

Generally well received by the critics, the Hopper-directed film is a crime picture starring Don Johnson (the king of the TV series *Miami Vice*), Virginia Madsen, and young Jennifer Connelly. Also starring was the soundtrack heavy on the country blues sound. In *The Washington Post*, Desson Howe ended his article this way: "*Hot Spot* will never go down as timeless, neoclassic noir. But, with its Hopperlike moments, over-the-top performances and infectious music, it carries you along for a spell."

"Contagious music," the critic wrote. And how! Composed by Jack Nitzsche (who contributed the sound-track to

Miloš Forman's *One Flew over the Cuckoo's Nest* and Taylor Hackford's *An Officer and a Gentleman*) and unfortunately underused in the movie, *The Hot Spot*'s music features both John Lee Hooker's laconic guitar riffs and threatening grumbling and Miles' melancholy, broken trumpet phrasings in a series of brush strokes on a blue canvas. Then it adds a secret ingredient: Taj Mahal on the dobro. The result is an atmospheric, almost dream-like album that stands among the best of either Hooker or Davis.

One element serves as the link between all of Miles' stylistically different periods, and that's his fidelity to the blues that he heard as a child in Saint Louis. This remained true, despite his joking rejoinder from the end of the 1960s, when white blues rock was emerging: "You know what? We're not going to play the blues anymore. Let the white folks have the blues. They've got the blues? Well, they can keep them!" But whatever the context, from be-bop to cool, hard bop to orchestral, modal, jazz rock, and everything in between, Miles' sound has always kept a tint of blue.

Then came the offer of his first real big-screen part, no doubt something of an accident. Australian director Rolf de Heer first considered Yaphet Kotto, then Sammy Davis Jr. to play the role of trumpeter Billy Cross, the hero of his 1991 film *Dingo*. According to the story, a friend of his suggested Miles whom he knew only by reputation, and certainly not as an actor.

Dingo is the tale of John "Dingo" Anderson who lives in the middle of the Australian bush, miles from nowhere. One day, when he is a kid, the private jet of American trumpeter Billy Cross makes an emergency landing in the middle of the desert for mechanical repairs. Accompanied by his musicians, Billy Cross offers a mini-performance for the lucky few spectators who happen to be there strictly by chance. Dingo is one of them, and he immediately falls under the jazzman's spell.

Afterward, as the band members are packing up their instruments, the boy gathers his courage to talk to the star. It was the best music he ever heard, he tells him. In front of the star-struck boy, Cross issues an invitation: "If you ever come to Paris, look me up." Then the side cargo door closes like an eye over the musician, and the plane takes off in a cloud of red and gold dust. The bug has bitten Dingo. Moved by a burning passion for Cross and his music, the boy will spend the next years mastering the trumpet, hoping to catch up to his idol one day and play alongside him. Which, of course, will happen – we are at the movies, after all.

Dingo is not a great film. That's the least we can say. It can't be compared to Bertrand Tavernier's *Round Midnight* that also features a veteran jazzman (sax player Dexter Gordon) who had no acting experience. Despite his weakness as an actor, Davis manages to create a larger than life character for Billy Cross, probably because the role was designed for him. Wallace Roney, Davis' friend and protégé, was aware of the film's shortcomings, yet in a conversation I had with him, he remarked, "I loved every scene he was in. It was completely him!" In one such scene, Dingo as an adult is questioning Billy Cross about some of his wrong career choices and his wariness about the media. "After playing the same old shit for 40 years, my soul had pulled a switch on me," the older man says in his distinctive gravelly voice. "I was becoming a jazz museum piece."

Miles was also asked to do the music for the film. Surprise – he turned to his old friend Michel Legrand and asked him to do the honors. In the liner notes of a recent reissue of *Legrand Jazz*, his 1958 record made in France, Legrand recalls how, a year before he died, Miles called him in Paris and invited him to come to Los Angeles to make a film soundtrack together. They spent their time doing everything but composing, to the point that Legrand accused him of being lazy. But at the last minute – no surprise – Miles pulled the rabbit out of the hat. Strange, Legrand reminisces, my first jazz record was with him, and his last jazz record was with me.

∾

Though director Clint Eastwood excluded Miles from his biopic *Bird* (1988) about Charlie Parker, which was strange given that Miles had been a close collaborator of Parker's during the finest years of the latter's career, the trumpeter had great potential as a subject and screen personality. Robert Budreau understood that completely, which is why he set out to film his story with Jamaican actor Kedar Brown playing him – the idol, rival, and denigrator of poor Chet Baker – in the movie *Born to Be Blue*, from 2015.

This anecdote tells us all we need to know about the problematic relationship between Miles and Chet, though Budreau didn't make it part of his movie. In 1952 and 1953, *DownBeat* magazine named Chet best trumpeter of the year, bypassing virtuosos like Dizzy Gillespie, Clifford

Brown, and, of course, Miles Davis. The first time they met in 1953 at the Lighthouse Café in Hermosa Beach, California, a contrite Chet Baker told Davis he was thinking about writing him a letter of apology, since he knew he wasn't up to his level. To which Miles answered, "If you ask me, you got about 15 other letters to write."

For years, Hollywood contemplated a film about Davis' life and career. A parade of producers, directors, screenwriters, and actors were named, or at least hinted at. In the early 1960s, Walter Yetnikoff, for a time the boss of Columbia Records, announced there would be a biopic drama starring Wesley Snipes as the trumpeter. The film rights for Davis' autobiography were bought and serious discussions with none other than Spike Lee began, but the production, whose working title was *Million Dollar Lips*, never saw the light of day.

Instead, the project piloted by actor Don Cheadle got the green light. Cowritten, coproduced, and directed by Cheadle, who also played the starring role, *Miles Ahead* (2015) portrays two parallel periods of the trumpeter's life. First, his reclusive years, far from stage and studio, from 1976 to 1981, and his moments of glory, tied to his tumultuous relationship with his first wife, dancer Frances Taylor. A British journalist seeks him out in his semi-retirement in hopes of interviewing him for *Rolling Stone*. Miles recruits the intruder to help him recover the original tapes for an eventual next record from an unscrupulous producer who has apparently stolen them.

Directed and acted with a certain assurance, *Miles Ahead* avoids most of the traps and clichés that weigh down

Hollywood biopics. Like Miloš Forman's *Amadeus* (1984) and *Born to Be Blue*, the screenplay presents a kind of reverie around the subject rather than a faithful portrait of factual reality. A legitimate choice, though some would have preferred a different tack. Anyone who has read the many biographies about the man, or even his tell-all autobiography, knows his life is scattered with moving, dramatic, and juicy anecdotes, numerous enough to fill a never-ending feature film or a season-length TV series. Knowing that, we may well wonder why the greater part of this movie was made up of endless chase scenes and guns going off, worthy of the most mediocre Blaxploitation pictures from the 1970s.

The problem with *Miles Ahead* is not the choice of fiction over the subject's reality. After all, on stage as on screen, *Amadeus* proved that a story can be created around a musician's life that captures their grandeur and weaknesses without strictly sticking to historical reality. The invented story has to present continuous interest, which is not the case with *Miles Ahead* any more than *Born to Be Blue*. In an off-the-cuff comment, trumpet player Wallace Roney, considered to be Miles' heir, told me, "If you're going to portray him as a gangster, at least make him a good gangster."

In other words, the definitive movie portrait of the musician remains to be made. To succeed, it will have to be sketched out in half tones subtle enough to correspond to his inspiration and his universe. Tones shadowed by the blues. But not just the blues.

Kind of blue, you might say.

Black and Blue (III)

After the partial victory symbolized by the Civil Rights Act of 1964, the influence of the pacifist movement subsided, while that of Black separatist organizations like the Nation of Islam increased. As the 1960s came to an end, even Black dance music moved from the convivial Motown soul to a more energetic, more rhythmic, and "darker" funky sound. More and more jazz artists joined the Black Power movement and filled their music with Afrocentrism, cultural revolt, and ethnic pride.

As Philippe Carles and Jean-Louis Comolli suggested in their work *Free Jazz/Black Power* (UBC Press and the University Press of Mississippi, translated by Grégory Pierrot), jazz has always been divided between two types of expression. One carries the African American collective memory, made of rage and imprecations, insults and blows, received throughout history and returned in musical form. The other was created to entertain the public, aimed to curry favor from white, upper-class critics, standardized in its forms of cultural colonialism. Starting from this point of view, Carles and Comolli sought to show where this music was made, the influences it was under, and the forces it pushed against. For the two authors, the free jazz artists who wanted to deconstruct the conventions used to define jazz were directly inspired by the militant current of thought represented by the Black Panthers. The dialectic between liberated jazz and the other kind born of compromise and popular consumption is illustrated by two archetypes. On one hand, there is the minstrel show, a white entertainer in blackface performing imitation African American music that led to vaudeville and eventually popular jazz. On the other, there is the bluesman, the solitary voice whose lamentation speaks to the ever-evolving movement of jazz.

These two European commentators, as well as another, Olivier Roueff, are worth lending an ear to. Roueff underscores the socially involved nature of free jazz artists, creators of a music that was conceived to be political from the very first note. They imbued their works with a sense of racial belonging, even if few of them directly participated in the civil rights movement or the Black Panther Party.

In September of 1968, the godfather of soul James Brown declared, "Say it loud – I'm Black and I'm proud!" Jazzmen would soon take up the same theme. Pianist Jaki Byard, a former member of Charles Mingus' band, recited the slogan on his *Jaki Byard Experience*, a record that came out on the Prestige label a few weeks after Brown's 45 hit the charts. The words ran like a litany at the beginning of his piece "Parisian Thoroughfare." The following year, saxman Lou Donaldson, an ex-Jazz Messenger who became a champion of soul jazz, gave his own reading of the song on his album *Say It Loud!* (Blue Note, 1969).

There's no underestimating the impact of James Brown's shouted declaration on subsequent generations of African Americans. "'Say it loud – I'm Black and I'm proud' was a record that really convinced me to say I was Black instead of a Negro," said rapper Chuck D of Public Enemy in an interview with *Mojo*. "Back then Black folks were called Negroes, but James said you can say it loud: that being Black is a great thing instead of something you have to apologize for." As part of his move into soul, funk, and psychedelic rock, Miles Davis sampled the bass line of Brown's song in "Yesternow" on his *Jack Johnson* documentary soundtrack (Columbia 1971).

As Cornel West pointed out in the prestigious French periodical *Le Monde diplomatique* in 1983, from the end of the 60s, "Black popular music took on more political intonations":

> With the intensification of the Vietnam War (more than 28% of American casualties were Black), drug culture spread while more Blacks were being elected to office. Recordings like the Temptations' "Ball of Confusion," the Chi-Lites' "Give More Power to the People," James Brown's (him again!) "Funky President (People, It's Bad)," and "Fight the Power" by the Isley Brothers displayed greater interest in public life and political participation among Afro-Americans.

Pride was the order of the day. No more bowing down. From their first day as an organization, the Black Panthers were dedicated to denouncing police brutality toward Black people in Oakland, California. But they were more than that. In 1969, they added community social programs to their core activities, such as free breakfasts for children and public health clinics. The Party recruited most of its members in the San Francisco Bay area but also spawned groups in urban centers: Chicago, Los Angeles, New York, Seattle, and Philadelphia.

Though outside jazz – but not too far outside – and in the same spirit of political and community activism, The Last Poets came together on May 19, 1968, in Harlem's Marcus Garvey Park to commemorate Malcolm X's birthday. The first version of the collective, whose members cycled in and out and occasionally changed their noms de guerre, included Abiodun Oyewole, Felipe Luciano, Gylan Kain, and David Nelson. They would soon make a name for themselves with their visceral poetry spoken over a background of throbbing percussion. On "allmusic.com," critic Jason Ankeny would write, "With their politically charged raps, taut rhythms, and dedication to raising African American consciousness, The Last Poets almost single-handedly laid the groundwork for the emergence of hip-hop."

No, not single-handedly. People often wrongly believe that the Watts Prophets, a group that came out of the Los Angeles ghetto, where the famous August 1965 riots erupted, walked in the footsteps of The Last Poets. But the Prophets were working long before the Poets emerged with their first record. The LA group was out to move a multiethnic audience with a more universal sound than the Poets, and though they were concerned with the needs and preoccupations of their immediate community, their songs spoke of the ongoing revolution in and around greater Los Angeles. At first a trio made up of Amde Hamilton, Richard

Dedeaux, and Otis O'Solomon (at the time named Otis Smith), the Prophets became a quartet with the arrival of pianist and singer Dee Dee McNeil on their first official album, *Rappin' Black in a White World* (1971). McNeil was a songwriter and composer from Detroit who had worked on the Motown assembly line, having had a hand in numbers by the Supremes, Edwin Starr, and David Ruffin. She would give *Rappin'* a new cohesion as well as change the Prophets' vocal dynamic. Her singing communicates both vulnerability and authority, and her voice turns fiery when she establishes certain basic truths: "Honey, there's a difference between a Black man and a nigger." The word *rap*, by the way, is attached to the Prophets who introduced it to refer to their form of poetic expression, even using it in the title of their first album. At the beginning of their shows, they often warned the audience, "We're going to rap you!"

In that same movement, we have to include poet, novelist, and militant Gil Scott-Heron, whose first album, *Small Talk at 125th and Lenox* (Flying Dutchman/RCA, 1970), was called "a volcanic upheaval of intellectualism and social critique" by John Bush (allmusic.com). On the record is the first version of his poem "The Revolution Will Not Be Televised," recited over a background of conga and bongo drums. A second more musical version came out the next year, with an unforgettable counterpoint from jazz flautist Hubert Laws and the melodic backup of a full orchestra. It would be the B side of the 45 "Home Is Where the Hatred Is" from the album *Pieces of a Man* (Flying Dutchman/RCA, 1971).

On a much more pop note, Marvin Gaye, the prince

of Motown who once tried to assume the identity of a jazz crooner in the style of Frank Sinatra and Nat King Cole, put out his landmark album *What's Going On* with Motown in 1971. The record was a turning point not only in his career, but in Motown's evolution and the history of Black popular music. With a fusion of soul, jazz, and classic tunes, his lyrics take on drugs, poverty, racism, political corruption, ecology, and the Vietnam War. Through nine songs, Gaye expresses the point of view of a soldier coming home to the country he fought for, only to find injustice, suffering, and hate. The inspiration was undoubtedly Marvin's brother Frankie who returned to civilian life again after three years of military service.

The record almost never happened. Al Cleveland and Renaldo Benson from the vocal group The Four Tops convinced Marvin Gaye to record the song "What's Going On" that they had co-written and co-composed with him. The boss of Motown, Berry Gordy, did not want to release it as a 45. He believed that a political song would be a commercial flop. But Gaye persisted, and the fact that he was Gordy's brother-in-law must have played in his favor. The song came out as a single and went on to be the fastest selling 45 in the label's history. It stood at the top of the R & B charts for five weeks and crossed over to the pop charts to take the number two spot. Comforted by this success, Gordy encouraged the production of an entire album in the same vein. The magazine *Billboard* listed it among the bestsellers for a whole year and a half with more than two million copies sold by the end of 1972. *What's Going On* was not only a commercial triumph; it took its place as one of the most important and influential pop music records of the twentieth century – the *Kind of Blue* of soul music.

Then there was LeRoi Jones who was many things, even before he took the name Amiri Baraka ("spiritual leader") the day after Malcolm X's assassination. He was a major figure of the Beat Generation, a militant, journalist, poet, playwright, novelist, and publisher. He founded Totem Press in 1958, which helped Kerouac and Ginsberg get their start. Today, he is best known for his essays and polemical writings. In 1972, he recorded the most atypical album in the Motown catalogue, *It's Nation Time* (Black Forum). The piece mixes soul, free jazz, tribal rhythms, chanting, poetry, and spoken word. There is even a deeply personal take on "Come See about Me," the hit popularized by The Supremes. Baraka repeats the melodic line and the central phrase like an incantation, which becomes a background to his own recitation.

Eight records came out between 1970 and 1973 on the Black Forum label. They are exceedingly rare items nowadays, and no Motown anthology ever included a single track from any of them. Among the sides, there is a Martin Luther King speech denouncing the Vietnam War, a fiery Stokely Carmichael sermon about race relations in the United States, a collection of interviews between *Time* journalists and Black soldiers in Vietnam... And then we come to this Amiri Baraka record whose pièce de résistance "Who Will Survive America?" begins with these words, rapped over a repetitive bass line:

Who will survive America?
Few Americans, very few Negroes, and no crackers at all.

A female chorus responds by taking up the words like a prayer, an obsessive mantra. Then the band breaks in with a funky style that conjures up Sly and the Family Stone. More ferocious than ever, Baraka picks up the microphone:

Will you survive America with your 20-cent habit?
Your fo' bag jones
Will you survive in the heat and fire of actual change?
I doubt it.

In an interview with the *African American Review* in 2003, Baraka explains the mix of influences that makes *It's Nation Time* what it is:

We were obviously digging Martha and the Vandellas and digging Smokey, just like we were digging Albert Ayler, Ornette Coleman and Trane. To us it was just different voices in the same family, different voices in the same community. The screaming and hollering in James Brown and the screaming and hollering in Albert Ayler was the same scream and hollering.

Not surprising that, at the time, a growing number of African Americans artists wanted to simply get rid of the name "jazz." They saw it as a leftover from the days of slavery. "If we continue to call our music jazz, we must continue to be called niggers," sax player Archie Shepp declared. He was echoing the arguments of drummer Max Roach, speaking in the magazine *Black World* in 1972:

We must cleanse our minds of false categories which are not basic to us, and which divide us rather than unite us. Regardless of what they are called (jazz, R&B, blues, etc.), they are various expressions of black music, black culture itself, the expressions of Africans in the diaspora. Yet black musicians are placed in these categories... and they face financial success or failure depending upon the popularity of their classifications at a given time.

In the middle of the 1960s, trumpeter Lee Morgan had phenomenal popular success with an album called *The Sidewinder* (Blue Note, 1964). The title piece sounded like a manifesto for jazz soul. Then he came under John Coltrane's influence. His music made a radical turn and he began exploring new, more political tangents on the record *Search for the New Land* (Blue Note, 1964), dedicated to the Nation of Islam. There were other such pieces taking the same direction: "Zambia" on *DelightfuLee* (Blue Note, 1967), "Afreaka" and "The Cry of my People" on *The Sixth Sense* (Blue Note, 1970). In 1970, Morgan and multi-instrumentalist Rahsaan Roland Kirk led a group of militant musicians on a number of projects under the name Jazz and People's Movement. They wanted to bring attention to the under-representation of jazz and its Black players on American television. They would slip into the audiences during the peak periods of talk shows and interrupt them to demand more jazz on the small screen.

A memorable sequence from the documentary *I Called Him Morgan* shows Lee with his group on the TV show

Soul during the 1971-1972 season. Their lead-off piece was "Angela," a composition by bassist Jymie Merritt dedicated to "Sister Angela Davis." At the time, the writer and militant feminist, once associated with the Black Panthers, was jailed for supposed terrorist activities. The piece would be included on *The Last Session* (Blue Note, 1972), issued in the spring following Morgan's tragic death.

All the same, during those years, creative African American music was slowly being pushed aside by more commercial forms. Despite that tendency, Atlantic Records, the label that had launched Ornette Coleman's career, dared to issue *Bap-tizum* (1972) by the Art Ensemble of Chicago, a young avant-garde group that came together in 1969 in the Windy City. There were some big names: Roscoe Mitchell on sax, Lester Bowie on trumpet, and Malachi Favors on bass. The record featured their live performance on stage at the Ann Arbor Jazz and Blues Festival, and the piece opened with a speech by militant John Sinclair. Politics was definitely on the menu.

Since the record industry generally had little interest in the avant-garde, pianist Stanley Cowell and trumpeter Charles Tolliver started their own co-op label, Strata-East. Pushed back to the underground by jazz rock that would occupy the media for a good part of the decade, free jazz still managed to prosper on the discreet loft scene. A number of discs emerged under the militant sign of Afrocentrism. There was Cowell's *Musa: Ancestral Streams* (Strata-East, 1973), Tolliver's *Live in Tokyo* (Strata-East, 1973), Cecil Taylor's *Akisakila* (Trio, 1973), and *A Message from the Tribe* by saxman Wendell Henderson and trombonist Phillip Ranelin.

Meanwhile, on his *Space Is the Place* from 1974, the iconoclastic jazz band leader Sun Ra was exhorting African Americans to leave Earth on the wings of his psychedelic music and travel to a new planet, free of the corrupting influence of white American society. The proposal echoed Marcus Garvey's fantasy of a return to Africa.

A Few Choruses from
Christian Gailly

From the very first pages of *Le Jazz, à la lettre: la littérature et le jazz* (2010), a collection of articles from various journals, Yannick Séité, a French academic, laments the fact that the music in question, though recognized as one of the essential art forms of the 20th century, is largely ignored in intellectual circles. He goes on to admit that jazz interests him less as an object of discourse among critics and writers and more when it inspires other artistic works that do not necessarily describe the music. Speaking against the poor quality of "jazzy" writing, Séité boldly maintains that "by following certain pathways, we might be able to come up with a list of works that authentically swing, though jazz is not present in them, though on the stylistic level, yes, perhaps."

Paradoxically (or nonsensically?), along with 20th-century writers like Louis-Ferdinand Céline and Jacques Réda, Séité offers up French wordsmiths from the distant past, from Montaigne to Villon and Saint-Simon, from Claudel to Chateaubriand who, so he says, have a certain jazziness in their writing. The paradox? Those great pens from centuries past never heard the music. At least Séité doesn't systematically discount everything that, in writing, may refer to music. He mentions "a certain use of repetition" in Philippe Soupault's poem "Georgia" from 1927 and Kerouac's choruses in *Mexico City Blues*, as well as Céline's "famous three-dot ellipses" that come close to "jazz syncopation," characteristic of the music's physicality. Séité believes in a metaphorical system that aligns jazz with the literary renewal of the second half of the 20th century. And this is because jazz symbolizes a revolt against certain rules of classical music as, in parallel fashion, literature adopted a new impulsive nature with language experimentation. Again, the academic cites Louis-Ferdinand Céline, reviled for his anti-Semitism and collaboration with the Nazis…

I have no idea if Séité ever got interested in the books of French novelist Christian Gailly. I looked in vain for an article by the former about the latter. Too bad. Gailly wrote novels with an absolute need for harmony and a perfect mastery of form, in which primary importance is given to rhythm and breath.

Gailly was born in Paris in 1943 into a family of modest means, and he was 44 when he published his first novel, *Dit-Il* ("He Says"), with Éditions de Minuit, a select, forward-looking publishing house run by a man named Jérôme Lindon. Gailly passed away at age 70, on October 4, 2013. In his 2007 book *Les Oubliés*, he readily owns up to the influence Samuel Beckett had on him:

> When I read the first page of *The Unnamable*, I felt like Beckett had stepped out of nowhere. He had given

himself permission to write the way he wanted to, not in relation to what had been done before. I even thought, naively, that he could have been illiterate! That's when I told myself, So, it *is* possible.

Although he claimed he wrote only for his friend and mentor whom he called "Monsieur Lindon," Gailly earned the faithful admiration of his readers. Though they weren't numerous at the start, the critics were enthusiastic and the juries followed suit. He won the France Culture prize for *Nuage rouge* ("Red Cloud") in 2000 and two years later, *Un soir au club* ("One Evening at the Club") picked up the Livre Inter prize. The cash registers began to sing: 170,000 copies sold. Even better, his work, 13 novels, an autobiography, and a story collection, had admirers in the film world. *Un soir au club* was made into a movie directed by Jean Achache in 2009, and that same year, Alain Resnais adapted *L'Incident* into the feature *Wild Grass*.

In November 2009, after the film debuted at the Cannes festival, Alain Resnais, well known for having directed *Hiroshima Mon Amour* and *Same Old Song*, spoke to journalist Olivier Delcroix from the daily *Le Figaro* about how the lively comedy based on *L'Incident* got turned into *Wild Grass*:

> Christian Gailly's style, his words, sentences, metaphors, they're constantly being telescoped. When I found out Gailly was a sax player in a little band, I understood I had the right tone, I suddenly began hearing jazz in his stylistic thrusts, the jumps of his time structure, his short circuits between past, present, and future.

Literary history abounds with examples of late-blooming yet enviable vocations. Like many such writers, Gailly did not seem destined to be a novelist. Quite the contrary. He did not grow up with books, and until his late twenties, despite having studied anthropology, linguistics, and psychoanalysis, literature remained a *terra incognita* for him. He discovered jazz when he was 16 and dreamed of being a musician. He played the tenor sax and nearly became a professional, but threw in the towel after a dozen years or so, in 1968. For the next three years, he worked installing and fixing central heating systems. He is quite clear about his musical talent in a 2002 interview with the Paris daily paper *Libération*:

> An amateur musician can never deliver the necessary kind of work with their instrument. That's the difference between an amateur and a professional. It was impossible to make a living with music. I wanted to be an excellent musician, I had a certain talent, my friends thought I was exceptionally gifted, but they weren't musicians. I've met some great players. You can look around, there's not a single saxophone in this house.

In 1971, Gailly picked up his saxophone again, then threw in the same towel a short time later. Journalist Nathalie Crom drew his portrait for the weekly culture magazine *Télérama* in 2007; the piece was dusted off after his death in 2013. This quote of his gives a possible reason for giving up: "After trying out free jazz and finding a terribly desperate and fleeting pleasure with it, I decided to abandon music altogether." After putting his sax away once and for all, Gailly dedicated himself to psychoanalysis.

His initial ambition to be a jazzman can be seen in his writing. Of course, his themes and contexts are drawn from music, but there's more: the rhythmic structure, the sound of it. Music is everywhere in his work. Mozart's presence is clear in *K.622* (1989), in which a pair of characters move toward the harmony of love as they listen to one of Amadeus' concerti together. Bach is present with his "Well-Tempered Clavier" in *L'Air* (1991) and his "Goldberg Variations" in *Dring* (1992). A more recent work, *Dernier amour* (2004), retraces a composer's return to his seaside house after a failed concert at a festival.

The bond between music and novel-writing is fundamental for Gailly. The second creative practice let him recover the first. In any case, his quotes from the Nathalie Crom piece point us in that direction:

> I realized right away that writing satisfied my old temptation to compose. When I manage to articulate a sentence in a way that satisfies me, the pleasure is like what a composer might feel. In that way, writing is the extension of my musical activity that never got anywhere.

That said, Gailly understands how difficult it is to transcribe music into prose, and he says as much in *K.622*:

> I'd like to be able to translate music, but it's impossible, I can't put music into words, it goes too fast, and I feel

desperate. But I try anyway, I start over again, it's no use, it doesn't work, if it's possible to put words into music, the opposite isn't true for me, music won't put up with a single word, it spits them out.

We can almost hear the echo of what Miles Davis said: "Don't write about the music, man. The music speaks for itself." Yet in his sixth novel, *Be-bop* (1995), Gailly lets himself be reborn as a jazzman.

When the book came out, Gilles Anquetil, a critic from the well-regarded magazine *Nouvel Observateur*, pointed out,

> There is a certain Gailly tone. A way of phrasing, casual and musical, leaping from one subject to the next, bringing together ideas, orderly and disorderly, that just seem to come to him.

When it came to the natural music of Gailly's phrasings in *Be-bop*, critic Jean-Noël Pancrazi went one step further in his article in the daily paper *Le Monde*. His comments were so favorable they ended up on the subsequent paperback edition of the novel:

> [...] syncopated syntax, continual tempo changes, interjections pronounced like lost, solitary notes, questions left hanging, apostrophes sometimes fraternal, other times mocking, addressed by the author to his character, abrupt returns to interior monologue, multiple, breathless hypotheses that Lorettu makes about

where he will go next, or directions he regrets having taken.

The book gives its writer, now in his fifties, a chance to reconcile with the young musician he once was. In *Be-bop*, the novelist weighed down by doubt extends a hand, in a manner of speaking, to the frustrated saxophonist who has gone silent. Gailly is a virtuoso with rhythm, repetitions and returns, sound and onomatopoeia. His title sets the stage: he is fond of alliteration with "b" and "p."

Be-bop is divided into three parts. In the theater, we would talk about acts. Here, we would say movements, as in a musical composition. Each of them starts off with a want ad. A job offer that the hero is supposed to react to, a rental announcement for a villa in the Savoy region, and the invitation to a concert at the monastery where the characters will join forces.

Before we reach that point, the novel introduces us to Basile Lorettu, a jobless young man who plays saxophone in the manner of Charlie Parker, even if his appearance is closer to that of another musician. "He has blond hair cut short like Mulligan," Gailly writes. "He looks like Gerry Mulligan and he knows it." Lorettu continually wrestles with a certain feeling of shame as he tries to appropriate the style and repertoire of his idol as faithfully as possible, convinced that "it's better to copy a great one like Charlie rather than try and be a great yourself and fall short."

And then, one night while playing at the Bird, his friend Fernand's club (the friend is a total Coltrane fanatic), Lorettu starts improvising for real on a Charlie Parker theme. Little by little, he pulls away from the real world, far from reality, and his saxophone starts to panic.

In the next passage, the tempo is still double time, but with a kind of lag, he starts wandering through the harmonies, scratching at the neighboring chords, the parallels and laterals, he widens them out, stretches them to the breaking point, it comes easily, he wants to show the others how far he's come, it gets more and more complex, the pianist is having trouble keeping up, like Tommy Flanagan chasing after Coltrane in "Giant Steps," but Nassoy [the bassist] follows perfectly, he figures why not and goes after the high range like a cello, Claude the drummer follows him, too, his replies are just right, magnificent.

Jazz, and Gailly knows it, is the ability to embrace the unexpected, open the door, and let it in. What comes next is not surprising:

Lorettu drops the harmonies, the rhythm, the structure – everything. His sax starts bellowing like a beast. It whimpers, cries, barks, hoots, cackles, screams. He hears its cries. Answers its own cries with others even more strident. Claude follows him but the other two have no idea what to do. Being so free so suddenly frightens them. In the end they stop playing.

This intense scene should be set side by side with the "terribly desperate and fleeting pleasure" that Gailly the saxophonist experienced during an amateur jazz festival in Zurich in 1964. The experience itself obviously had consequences on the future novelist, as he told it to a journalist who interviewed him for the "L'Oreille absolue" blog.

> That evening, I completely abandoned the harmonic and rhythmic structure. It wasn't the first time we played that way. [...] Slowly, the audience began to react. They protested, as a joke people answered by imitating the sounds my sax made. I returned the favor, I blew like hell into my tenor. It ended in a veritable cataclysm of sound. After five minutes, the audience was yelling so loud the organizers decided to bring down the curtain. It turned into a riot... You can imagine what I felt when I went back and wrote and experienced all that again.

Gailly himself admitted that this half-page text hardly gives a true idea of what he went through.

> When we found ourselves behind the lowered curtain... The musicians were not in very good shape and I was in tears. Driven by the music, despite myself, suddenly I had to fight an audience that, in its stupidity, incarnated an esthetics of opposition, everything that stood against a band like ours.

But fiction is there to redeem the biographical past. The audience at the Bird club does not shout down Basile Lorettu. On the contrary. When the sax player emerges from his trance, he gets all sorts of reactions: laughter, timid applause, whistling. Our hero realizes he's locked eyes with a woman in the club, Cécile, who is there with her daughter. He takes the instrument from around his neck, sets it on the piano, and, without thinking twice, steps down from the stage and moves toward the woman. And though they soon begin seeing each other, Cécile remains distant and reserved with him, unlike her daughter, who makes it clear she is ready for romance. Sparks fly between her and Basile, almost by accident one night after he has had dinner at her place, even if Cécile is the one he wants. This engaging non-description of their little tango is typical of Gailly's brand of humor:

Lorettu's place. Ah there's the famous sax, Cécile's daughter says, picking up the alto lying on the bed. Oh, it's so heavy. She doesn't know where to put her fingers. Like this, Lorettu says. She blows hard. Lorettu looks at her round lips. She takes the sax in her mouth like a penis. Soon she'll be doing the same with him. But if the scene bothers you, we can just as well cut it. Okay, it's gone. Though it did happen.

Lorettu is troubled – he's a creature of habit. Each day, his routine goes like this: wake up in the morning, practice his horn, cut himself shaving, jump into his Air Jordan rap version of seven-league boots, buy the paper, have a quick drink at the Bird to the sound of the Coltrane records that never stop playing there, go out and take a stroll, sit on a park bench, think about Cécile who prefers Beethoven to jazz (but at least she likes reading him the want ads from the papers). The search keeps his mind busy. Then Lorettu will find a job, though not the most exciting, with a septic tank pumping company where he'll be in charge of shit-pumping, the perfect occupation for a lost soul divorced from the world around him.

One thing leads to another, and our hero ends up on the shores of Lake Geneva, in Switzerland, in a Savoyard villa whose plumbing is backed up. He makes the acquaintance of the August tenants, a couple in their fifties, Jeanne and her husband Paul Saint-Sabin. He once played tenor sax at a semi-professional level, but his taste for jazz and his love of taking risks have dried up. The book's atmosphere changes. Gailly abandons the flamboyant, staccato approach of the beginning for a more serene, fluid style that speaks to the quiet distress of the hero as he faces turning 50.

It's obvious that married life is slowly suffocating Paul. He doesn't know how to express his desire for Jeanne anymore, how to go about desiring her, even if she is splendid in her little flowered dress. Lorettu, the Gerry Mulligan look-alike, offers Paul a way out of his alienation and self-deprecation. Like all lovers of the blue note, they just need to hunker down and have a serious conversation about, for example, Mulligan's classic recordings during the golden years with Chet Baker on trumpet and Bob Brookmeyer on trombone. That will make all the difference, just one short conversation and Paul will feel like living again.

Fate being what it is, the two men will meet again.

Paul is curious. He wants to know whether Lorettu plays for fun or for real. He decides he's going to find out for himself. In the final movement of the novel, he goes to listen to the younger man's quintet during one of his Sunday concerts in the local monastery's crypt.

Suddenly the old days when Jeanne and Paul first met in a downstairs club don't seem too distant, even though that was 30 years back. He played tenor sax in a quartet and he played well, Jeanne and her sister were wild about jazz, and they ended up marrying the group's saxophonist and drummer.

The first set of their crypto-concert kicks off with an old Charlie Parker blues that everyone appreciates:

Applause and encouragement. "Now's the Time" makes everyone happy to be alive. After Patrick's intro, as soon as the saxes and trumpet move in, the audience goes crazy, shouting, whistling, getting to their feet, shaking it, sitting down again, dancing in their seats, clapping their hands, the two-one, two-one beat, some girls are snapping their fingers, long elegant fingers, of course, and biting their lower lip.

That's how the novel closes out, abruptly, on this note of reconciliation between us and the world, with music as the mediator.

∾

Gailly's structure in *Be-bop* and later in *Un soir au club* is quite close to the way Parker, Mulligan, Coltrane, and others interpreted the standards of the Great American Songbook: stating the theme, improvising with rich use of references, then returning to the initial theme. In an interview with *Libération*, the ex-saxophonist turned psychoanalyst explained:

> When I've got my scene in hand, and feel the story won't get away from me, I'm not afraid of coming at it in a disorderly way, saying what the end is, I know I won't lose my way. I've inherited a situation close to the pleasure of telling things out loud, with incidental clauses and digressions.

Un soir au club follows in the same vein as *Be-bop*, with its narrator being a painter and friend of the couple made up of Simon Nardis and his wife Suzanne. Though Simon had once been a renowned jazz pianist, he abandoned his career in music for health reasons and became an ideal husband: he listens only to classical music and hasn't touched a keyboard or a drop of drink in ten years. He has led the most peaceful and exemplary of lives... until one day, being a specialist in industrial heating, he travels to a seaside city to help an engineer get a factory back up and running.

The work at the factory is more laborious than expected, and he misses his train home. Since he has time before the next departure, he agrees to have dinner with the engineer. When the latter discovers that Simon is a jazz enthusiast, he offers to take him for drinks at the Green

Dolphin, a local club that takes its name from the standard popularized by Miles Davis and Bill Evans. A piano trio is playing there, "the finest group in Simon's estimation."

As he listens to the young house pianist revisit the standards, and quite skillfully at that, Simon is surprised to recognize his own style of piano playing. He decides he must have had something original about him if he inspired at least this one disciple. After a few drinks, the desire to sit down at the keyboard gets the better of him. As it so happens, the members of the trio are taking their break just then, and Simon has a few spare minutes before he needs to get to the station. He gathers his courage to sit down at the piano. At first his hands are trembling, but his nerves calm, and he feels more comfortable and forgets about the world around him. The music takes over. So much so that he misses his train again.

Drawn to Simon's playing and sure she knows him from somewhere, Debbie joins him on stage. "This could be the start of something big," she sings, the line from the old standard popularized by Mark Murphy.

There's just one small problem: Suzanne, Simon's wife, is back home waiting for him to show up. When Simon misses a few more trains the next day, she decides to go retrieve him in their car. She doesn't like seatbelts, and this time that will cost her her life.

Meanwhile, Simon savors his newfound happiness with Debbie and the return of music into his life – even if he does remember that he has a wife waiting for him. He calls her and promises to take the next train and tells her to wait for him. He doesn't consider staying with Debbie, even once he learns Suzanne is dead. The strange work of destiny.

In the evening, Simon's son reaches him on the phone to announce the tragic news. Two cars set out for the hospital where Suzanne's body lies, one with Simon's son, his girlfriend, and Suzanne's cat; the other with Simon and Debbie. The cat escapes a hundred kilometers from the hospital. The next time we see it, it's at Suzanne's side.

Gailly loves to use musical metaphors to describe situations that don't necessarily have anything to do with music. An example would be the exact moment when Simon Nardis learns of his wife's death:

> His reaction arose from the depths of space like dark, heavy notes, beating out in the lowest end of the scale, something like a Zen rumbling, moving to the higher register, a crescendo of profanity.

As I mentioned, in 2009 Jean Achache adapted the novel into a film that was remarkable in more than one way. First, the screenplay that he and Guy Zilberstein wrote betrays neither the spirit nor the letter of Gailly's book, remaining true to its plot and atmosphere. Also, the music scenes are played in a very convincing manner by Thierry Hancisse (an actor from the classical Comédie française) and Élise Caron, excellent in their roles as Simon Nardis and Debbie Parker, though at times they do seem too theatrical. What's more, the music composed by Franco-Algerian bassist Michel Benita is good quality stuff.

In his description of what he was aiming for with the

film, Achache talks about his work in terms that are in complete harmony with Gailly's esthetics:

> I made this movie because I love music. I made this movie because I love love stories. I made this movie because I love the lights that burn at night, I love the atmosphere of harbors, the empty streets, the landscapes left unoccupied. I made this movie about love and music in the port of Brest, at night, in the evening.

Some sour-minded people have criticized this rather bitter novel and the film based on it: its pacing is too slow, the main character is childish. There is no accounting for taste… I liked not only the music but the silences, very convincing and well used. We are watching characters who are more than a little lost and wondering what direction their lives will go.

To paraphrase Thelonious Monk, the pianist to whom we owe a hundred or so of the modern repertory's most major compositions, before you begin a chorus, before you play a single note, you have to be sure that that note is worth breaking the silence for.

Both Gailly the novelist and Achache the filmmaker seem to have taken Monk's advice.

In Love with the Night Mysterious

In love with the night mysterious
The night when you first were there

—"So in Love," words and music
by Cole Porter

When the film *De-Lovely* came out in 2004, it garnered diametrically opposed critical reactions. I for one believe that Irwin Winkler's biopic about composer Cole Porter is worth seeing and watching again and again. Porter, again in my opinion, is the most brilliant contributor to the Great American Songbook, the vast repertory of popular songs which jazz has returned to many times over. The famous TV host Larry King called the film "Far and away the best musical biography ever made." Meanwhile, Stephen Holden of *The New York Times* pitilessly claimed that the picture was "lethally inert" and "lifeless and drained of genuine joie de vivre," especially when compared to Ken Russell's surreal biopics of composers or any of Federico Fellini's libidinous self-portraits.

One thing's for sure: no admirer of Porter's sparkling songs could prefer the previous Hollywood production dedicated to the life and work of the songwriter-composer – the 1946 fantasy called *Night and Day*, directed by Michael Curtiz. The film starred Cary Grant, rumored to be bisexual among Hollywood circles, and at the time not yet associated with Hitchcock's cinema. Legend has it that Grant was hired at Cole Porter's suggestion. Marc Eliot, Grant's biographer, admits that this story of Porter's life, wiped clean of all references to his homosexuality (ah, those were the days…) was coolly received:

> Despite generally lukewarm reviews by skeptical critics, who knew better than to accept this version of Cole Porter's life as anything but Hollywood fantasy, everyone loved Grant's acting and even his campy singing in a memorable rendition of "You're the Top." Whenever Porter was asked how he felt about it, he insisted he loved the film as well, but he was always quick to qualify his opinion with the disclaimer that there wasn't a word of truth in it.

We can only speculate on what he would have thought about *De-Lovely*.

One engaging sequence of Irwin Winkler's film shows Porter, played in grand fashion by Kevin Kline, and his wife Linda (Ashley Judd is impeccable in the role) taking in a private screening of *Night and Day*. At the end of that movie, to the sound of the song that provided the title, pompously interpreted by a chorale, Linda (Alexis Smith), who has forgiven everything Cole (Cary Grant) has ever done, throws herself into her husband's arms. Version #2 of

Porter is incredulous, though moved, and can hardly keep his feet. "If I can survive this film, I can survive anything," says the Kline version of Porter who was handicapped after a serious horse-riding accident.

He and Linda are old and gray now, unlike the glamorous actors who played the parts in 1946. Despite his obvious physical pain as he goes down the stairs at the movie theater, Porter, still the bon vivant, casually discusses the whitewashing of their real lives that they have just watched.

> PORTER: Why on earth does Linda come back to Cole anyway?
> LINDA (jokingly): Because he's Cary Grant. (Then more seriously.) And she misses the music, as do I.
> PORTER: I must say, going down in history as Cary Grant is not too bad. Not for a boy from Indiana.
> LINDA: We should be grateful to them, they found us a happy ending.

A happy ending. And not just any kind…

Night and Day reinvents their story from the ground up with no concern for the chronology of events or whether they were true or not. Curtiz's film's screenplay had three authors: Charles Hoffman, Leo Townsend, and William Bowers. They decided that the rich divorcée Cole met in Paris would become a roommate to Nancy, Cole's cousin, who came to spend the holidays on the Porter clan's holdings in Peru, Indiana.

The scene can't help but make us smile. Logs burn in the

fireplace, snowflakes glitter at the window, and servants serve the guests gathered around the grand piano where young Cole, with his Yale diploma and who is now studying law at Harvard, is part of the Christmas 1914 festivities. With Nancy by his side, he sings "In the Still of the Night," culminating in the line "Are you my life-to-be, my dream come true?"

All during the song, his eyes are glued to Linda Lee's. True, he has just met her, but the way they gaze at each other is so intense that love will soon be blooming.

Just like in the movies.

Of course, Cole Porter wouldn't write "In the Still of the Night" until 1937, but this anachronism is the least of the film's missteps. In scene after scene, *Night and Day* takes such liberties with the story it is supposed to tell that it can hardly be called a biography.

Back in the big city, Porter officially quits his legal studies and opts for a life in the arts. With the help of his old friend Monty Woolley, who plays himself on screen (or more accurately, a heterosexual version of himself), Porter puts together his first musical, *See America First*. Nancy and her ravishing friend Linda Lee join in the production. Unfortunately, the show is interrupted by the announcement that a German submarine has just torpedoed and sunk the British ocean liner *RMS Lusitania*. That would make the next day May 7, 1915. But history tells us that this satirical patriotic opera, words and music by Porter with a libretto by T. Lawrason Riggs, was actually staged March 28, 1916, at the Maxine Elliott's Theater, where it hung on for 15 days.

After *See America First* failed, Porter left for Europe with the intention of seeing combat with the French

Foreign Legion, but he was soon wounded in action. Many biographies doubt whether he really did take part in the fighting. While recovering in a French hospital, he is reunited with Linda who has signed up as a nurse. To lift his spirits, she finds him a piano so he can go back to his art, and he gives birth to the song whose title will be the same as the film's title, as well as one of the most parodied scenes ever made. It involves Cary Grant at the piano reacting in real time to the sounds conjured up by the lyrics – the clock, the rain, and "a voice within me keeps repeating you, you, you."

Linda invites Cole to join her in a villa on the French Riviera, but he is reticent about accepting the rich heiress' money. Instead, he returns to New York to take up his work again. There, he finds a job playing piano in a music store. Tired of performing the same old songs, his partner, singer Carole Hill, tries out one of his compositions. He immediately hatches the idea of producing a new show, *The New Yorkers*, with his old pal Monty.

This time things go well, and Cole is invited to England to write another show. In London, he runs into Linda seemingly by accident, and they get together again, marry, and return to New York, where he begins working on yet another show. Cole promises many things to Linda, like going on a long voyage together, but his shows take up all his time. Tired of unfulfilled promises, she goes off to Europe to live alone.

Cole gets a phone call from his mother, telling him that his grandfather is on his deathbed. He returns to Indiana to reconcile with him. After the burial, during a storm, he is badly injured in an equestrian accident and loses the use of his legs. Cole makes Monty promise he won't breathe a word to Linda about his handicap. Will the two lovebirds ever be united?

Call it a case of false suspense.

The happy ending is right around the corner...

~

All that being said, there's no reason to believe that *De-Lovely* is any closer to reality than *Night and Day*. Both films are works of fiction and feature creative liberties that show how little the facts matter in such situations and how the interpretation of reality is what counts. Inspired by a multiplicity of sources, biopics are not made to inform. They are more about entertainment than anything else. They are an homage to a famous individual. They are out to shed new light on his or her story and usually have no pretensions of being documentaries.

I have had just this kind of discussion with my composer and pianist friend Anthony Rozankovic about Peter Shaffer's play *Amadeus* (1974). My colleague has no qualms about the factual liberties taken by both this successful play and Miloš Forman's excellent 1984 film adaptation, no more than he did about Alexander Pushkin's poetic drama *Mozart and Salieri* which was the inspiration for the two later works. If Rozankovic has any concerns, it's that these fictional stories, these representations, have entered the consciousness of too many people and become the truth about the relations between these two composers of the Viennese court.

Rumors did circulate at the time in Vienna claiming that Salieri really did poison Mozart. But history has never corroborated the whispered stories that Pushkin, then Shaffer based their works on. In no way can we prove that Salieri felt any particular envy or resentment toward his younger colleague.

De-Lovely differs from *Night and Day* in its organization and structure. The former begins in 1964 in the New York apartment where Cole Porter has been living as a recluse for several years. He has just died, and he knows it. (Actually, Porter died in Santa Monica, California, but let's not let the facts get in the way.) In the shadowy parlor, his wheelchair pulled up close to his piano, he puffs on a cigarette as he plays a few measures of his famous tunes, from "Night and Day" to "In the Still of the Night." He stops suddenly when he spots the supernatural apparition of what looks like the director, Gabe – Jonathan Pryce, in fine form. Gabe is here to take him to a show that is about to begin. The exchange between the two of them is a delight:

GABE: Hello, Cole. I let myself in.
PORTER: We're not late, are we? I hate to be late.
GABE: No, we're fine. (Referring to the tunes.) That sounded lovely.
PORTER: I hate funeral music. Though, under the circumstances, I suppose l should say my prayers.
GABE: Why start now?
PORTER: Exactly. lf I believed in God, he would be a song-and-dance man. He would have to carry a tune. (He gets back to playing the piano, the first bars of

"Let's Misbehave") Preferably one of mine. Do you think he would like this?

Gabe, who is none other than the Archangel Gabriel, has arrived to escort the late Porter to a theater where the salient facts of his tortured existence will be presented to him in a show. The common belief is that a person sees the scenes of their life flash by them in their last seconds. What could be more appropriate than for Cole Porter to have his life presented to him as a musical?

Transported to the theater by the magic of music – his own music – Porter looks on as a younger version of himself launches into "In the Still of the Night," but not loud enough for him. Astonished, he realizes he can't get the younger Porter to hear him. Gabe urges him to give his opinion, which he will transmit to the cast members. "Times have changed," he explains to the older Porter. At that very second, the younger version launches into "Anything Goes" whose first verse happens to be "Times have changed."

> GABE: (explaining his choice): Never open with a ballad.
> PORTER: This isn't one of those avant-garde things, is it? It's got to be entertaining, it's a musical.
> GABE: (insisting): And a love story, of course. A little unconventional, but honest.
> PORTER: (uneasy): You're playing with my life.
> GABE: (uncompromising): It's my show.

These lines would sound just as appropriate spoken by the director Irwin Winkler or his screenwriter Jay Cocks, who are running the game here. The lines also justify the film's anachronisms and inventions, since it is not aiming for a documentary approach. The film tells us that what matters is what's shown on screen, the artistic, subjective reenactment of Porter's existence, to which the late composer can object if he wishes.

Appearing from everywhere, from the last row of the gods to the wings, the story's characters step on stage with the young Cole Porter to interpret the standard so emblematic of the casual stance Porter affected. Then, last but not least, Linda Lee Porter (Ashley Judd) walks into the spotlight, and it is her turn to belt out a few lines from the song: "If old chairs you like / If backstairs you like / If love affairs you like."

The dead version of Porter protests for the first time. Those words don't work in Linda Lee's mouth. Gabe agrees and puts an end to the scene. Stopped cold, Linda wonders if she went astray. The director assures her that it has nothing to do with her. Then Gabe shoos away everyone who is not part of the next scene, which is a future couples first meeting at a wedding reception at the Ritz in Paris, January 30, 1918. And the show goes on...

Every time I watch the film, I appreciate how smoothly we move from the realistically filmed scenes of Cole and Linda's life and the conversations between Gabe and the dead Cole who are attending the reenactment in this little theater. Charmed by their first encounter, Linda, the wealthy divorcée, falls hard for Cole after a stroll through a park during which he sings "Easy to Love" to her. Of course she falls for this funny, talented, delicate, and charming man, despite the fact that he's ten years younger than she is. The film eliminates that aspect of their story by casting Ashley Judd, who is much younger than Kevin Kline. But why does she fall for him so quickly?

William McBrien came up with an explanation. He is the author of *Cole Porter: A Biography* (Knopf 1998), and offered this point of view to Robert F. Howe of *Smithsonian Magazine* after *De-Lovely* was released:

> Together they made a greater whole. They had a brilliant social life in the first years of their marriage, and someone once suggested to me that Cole Porter may have been well suited to Linda because women who are great beauties don't want to be mauled by men."

Remember that she had already divorced one man who apparently was violent with her. Besides being the perfect cover for his homosexuality at a time when a man absolutely needed one, Porter saw in her sophistication, security, and a way to satisfy his voracious social appetite. She saw in him a way to reach a new and foreign world. Music historian Stephen Citron also penned a Porter biography, *Noel and Cole: The Sophisticates* (Oxford University Press, 1993), and contributed this thought:

> What Linda wanted was to be a patron of the arts. She tried desperately to get Cole to compose classical music, which she thought was the entry into fame. She finally gave up that quest. She really loved him and

stuck by him because he was her passport to a kind of enduring fame.

Because she admired and loved Cole with all her heart, she married him at the City Hall of the 18th Arrondissement in Paris, her second try at tying the knot. She was perfectly aware of his sexual orientation. As for the subject, the first time he timidly brought it up leads to another delicate and juicy episode in the film. The couple is in the garden of Linda's stately residence. Linda is cutting flowers as Porter watches her, smoking a cigarette, with the look of someone walking on eggs.

PORTER: I've never had the urge to be completely honest with anyone until you. It's quite disturbing. Especially since I haven't been totally honest.
LINDA: (chuckling): You knew so much about me when we met, Cole... Don't you think I'd heard a thing or two about you?
PORTER: Then you know about... (Hesitatingly.) Well, that l can be... That I have... other interests. Interests, the pursuit of which some people might find cruel to you.
LINDA: You mean men?
PORTER: Yes, men.
LINDA: Let's just say you like them more than I do.
She sits down at the garden table, facing him.
LINDA: Nothing is cruel that fulfills your promise.
PORTER: I've been promising all my life. I've got a notebook full of promise. Trunks full. I want to be more than promising to you.

And so begins this love story made atypical by the fact that Porter does not desire Linda physically but appreciates the togetherness and intimacy they share. *De-Lovely* assumes the existence of a deep and real love, the kind Porter describes in "True Love." It is one of his most unusual songs, and we hear it in the film, interpreted as by the duo of Linda and Honoria Murphy, the daughter of a couple Porter is friends with.

"While I give to you and you give to me / True love, true love," they sing.

Then, this exchange: "Cole, I know this is your song, but it just doesn't sound like you," Sara Murphy points out to him. "Linda thinks it does," he answers, amused.

First sung by Grace Kelly and Bing Crosby in the 1956 film *High Society*, two years after Linda's death, "True Love" would earn Porter an Oscar nomination for best original song. Unfortunately for our hero, the statuette went to "Que Sera Sera" (Whatever Will Be, Will Be)" by Jay Livingston and Ray Evans, as sung by Doris Day in Alfred Hitchcock's *The Man Who Knew Too Much*.

Whatever the case, "True Love" does seem a bit out of place in a repertory generally characterized by irony, sensuality, outright expressions of lust, and obsessive, imperious desire – the kind that, though often fleeting, is comparable to a natural disaster. Examples? "I've Got You Under my Skin," "I Get a Kick Out of You," "Get Out of Town," "Night and Day," "Let's Do It," "Just One of Those Things," "Begin the Beguine," the unfairly neglected "Experiment," and others along the lines of "Let's Misbehave." Expressions of what F. Scott Fitzgerald called "the jazz age."

As for the pure, uncorrupted love described in "True Love" and love as a source of pain and confusion in "What Is This Thing Called Love?," Porter pretends to let the poets, with their "childish way," elucidate this mystery. Then he lets the young prostitute in the steamy "Love for Sale" take over, and she doesn't mince words:

And if you want the thrill of love
I've been through the mill of love
Old love, new love
Every love but true love

I rest my case.

When the song was first performed in *The New Yorkers* in 1930, the press accused "Love for Sale" of being in bad taste, and versions of it sung with the lyrics were banned from the radio waves. All the same, the 1931 recordings of it by Libby Holman and by Fred Waring's group The Pennsylvanians had some success. But we would have to wait until 1952 and for Billie Holiday, who was a prostitute when she was younger, before "Love for Sale" acquired some credibility. Besides Lady Day, most female singers and all male singers did not dare take on the song – it was judged to be too hot. That said, the instrumental versions by Sidney Bechet, Erroll Garner, Art Tatum, Charlie Parker, and Miles Davis made "Love" into a standard. Fortunately, the puritanical reading of it began to fade in the 1960s.

The opposite of representing Cole Porter as an inoffensive charmer of the ladies, and completely in tune with Cary Grant's reputation, *De-Lovely* went ahead and did something that was unthinkable in 1946. It represented the songwriter and composer as a full-fledged seducer of men, a shameless hedonist who featured sensual pleasure as a re-current theme of his songs. After all, birds do it, bees do it, even educated fleas do it...

Only when her husband's morals risk being brought into the glaring light of day and her standing as a respectable member of the bourgeoisie is imperiled does Linda protest with any kind of vehemence. After a blackmail artist extorts a considerable sum from them in exchange for not publishing compromising photos he took of Porter in a Hollywood bordello for men, things between the couple turn nasty.

> LINDA: You have put everything that you've accom-plished with your music at risk.
> PORTER: Darling, my work has never been better. It's flourishing. Even if we're not.
> LINDA: Your music comes from your talent, not from your behavior.
> PORTER: It's all the same thing. I can't put my talent here and my behavior here... and my eating, sleeping, and drinking habits. It's all me.
> LINDA: I have never asked you to change. Just be dis-creet.
> PORTER: Linda, I have never been discreet.

The detractors of *De-Lovely* went searching for faults. They called Linda's pregnancy and miscarriage a case of wholesale invention, whereas informed sources confirm the events. Does the film over-emphasize Porter's homosexuality, as some people maintained? In *Cole Porter: A Biography*, William McBrien doesn't hesitate to establish a link between Porter's work and his sexual orientation, basing his position on the steamy letters Porter wrote to his lovers:

> The passion here may startle those who know Porter only from the nonchalant persona he chose to present to society. But these words help those who are moved by Porter's songs to understand the origins of the ardor that is replicated in lyrics and in his throbbing rhythms and intoxicating melodies.

In his book about contemporary Hollywood biopics called *Whose Lives Are They Anyway?*, Dennis Bingham postulates that these kinds of movies analyze and question the historical importance of a famous personality by shining a spotlight on the subtleties of their character. It does not matter what they represented during their lifetimes. Their behavior, their action in private, and the public events they took part in are interpreted in spectacular fashion. At the heart of every biopic is the need to put the elements of the story into context. Not the subject's context – the current context of the director and the film.

For *De-Lovely*, the movie's producers used contemporary pop stars to create the soundtrack, which clearly proves Bingham's point. Featured were Robbie Williams and Vivian Green, Elvis Costello, Sheryl Crow, Lemar, Alanis Morissette, and others. Gabe, who wants to reassure Linda after the aborted opening number ("Anything Goes"), tells her, "Have you ever seen a musical without a happy ending?"

With those words, he is establishing the director's control over his film.

The movie's point of view and happy ending lie not so much in the end of the plot, which is foreshadowed from the very first scene, but in what the story says about Porter's life. Despite all his homosexual adventures, he loved only – really loved – Linda. No doubt the most moving sequence of the picture is trying to express just that. That's the one where we see Cole singing "So in Love" to Linda, who is crippled by emphysema and sitting next to him at the piano. Then comes a parallel scene: the widowed Cole alone at the premiere of *Kiss Me, Kate*, where the song is interpreted in almost operatic fashion by Mario Frangoulis and the enervating Lara Fabian.

And it doesn't matter that, in reality, *Kiss Me, Kate* previewed and ran for three weeks at Philadelphia's Schubert Theater starting December 2, 1948. Its official run began on December 30 and lasted for 19 weeks at the New Century Theatre, before returning to the Schubert for the next few months. Neither does it matter that Linda did not succumb to emphysema until May 20, 1954.

"It's my show," the Archangel Gabriel warns us, clearly speaking in the name of director Irwin Winkler.

Anyway, when it comes to Cole Porter, anything goes.

Black and Blue (IV)

"Time is running out" on Black power, The Last Poets prophesized in 1971 on *This Is Madness* (Douglas Records). The revolution that would not be televised, as Gil Scott-Heron insisted, did not seem to be showing up after all. Partly due to FBI interference and outright suppression, the Black Panther Party was in disarray. "Those who have the power always have the time and resources to get together," Umar Bin Hassan of the Last Poets would comment. "They took their blows for a minute but then they realized, 'We gotta come back at this.'" The man who ran the FBI for nearly half a century, J. Edgar Hoover, was famous for declaring that "the Black Panther Party, without question, represents the greatest threat to internal security of the country."

On Hoover's orders the FBI followed the "divide and conquer" strategy and created tensions between the Party's major figures, Huey Newton and Eldridge Cleaver, and between the different militant African American associations. "They tried to destroy and discredit the Black Panther Party by any means necessary," stated Emory Douglas, a painter and the Party's Minister of Culture. After receiving two grants from the National Endowment for the

Arts, the Watts Writers' Workshop, the Watts Prophets' headquarters, watched as the building that held its workshop and adjacent theater was burned and completely destroyed. The arsonist was Darthard Perry, an FBI mole who confessed to his activities in 1975.

On July 5, 1973, at the Montreux Jazz Festival in Switzerland, soul jazz diva Marlena Shaw gave a concert composed essentially of standards. But there was a twist at the end: she took a song off Marvin Gaye's *What's Going On*, "Save the Children." Then she added a ten-minute version of her hit "Woman of the Ghetto" that would be endlessly sampled during the hip-hop era. Everyone got into the act, including the British DJ Blue Boy ("Remember Me" on the soundtrack of the film *Forces of Nature*, DreamWorks, 1999); the French musician St Germain ("Rose rouge" on the album *Tourist*, Blue Note, 2000); and the rapper Ghostface Killah, former member of the Wu-Tang Clan ("Ghetto" on *Apollo Kids*, DefJam, 2010). A few lines of the song will take us back to those times:

> *How do you raise your kids in a ghetto?*
> *How do you raise your kids in a ghetto?*
> *Do you feed one child and starve another?*
> *Won't you tell me, legislator?*

The Party launched some excellent progressive initiatives. There was the free breakfast program for underprivileged children started in 1969. There were other community health and legal aid programs as well, and free shoes for the poor. Still, the ship was taking on water. On the musical front, after hearing Bill Calhoun and his friends singing harmony, Emory Douglas got the idea to start a funk group that would transmit the Party's ideology using original material or hit songs with new lyrics changed for the needs of the cause. He called the group The Lumpen, borrowing the term from Marx. But the internal divisions only worsened. In 1977, Elaine Brown, the first woman elected to lead the organization, quit after Huey Newton endorsed the beating of Regina Davis, a Party administrator. Eight years earlier, Brown recorded the Party hymn "The Meeting" on *Seize the Time* (Vault). It seemed like the moment had passed...

Despite the outright and covert repression of Black liberation movements and the record industry's disinterest in any music that was either too political or too steamy, the Afrocentrist tendency was still active among many artists through the 1970s. At the beginning of the decade, pianist Herbie Hancock adopted a Swahili name, Mwandishi, for himself and his jazz funk group. The members of the sextet all took on pseudonyms from the Bantu language of sub-Saharan Africa. Eddie Henderson (trumpet) became Mganga; Bennie Maupin (sax and clarinet) turned into Mwile; Julian Priester (trombone) chose Pepo Mtoto; Buster Williams (bass) went for Mchezaji; meanwhile drummers Billy Hart and Leon Chancler became Jabali and Ndugu respectively. After the group broke up, Hancock would go on to lead the Headhunters. Once a racist and pejorative designation, he stood it on its head as a mark of pride.

California sax player David Murray was part of the scene, too. He set up shop in New York in 1975 and rubbed shoulders with his avant-garde colleagues at the Rivbea Studio, a loft turned into a performance space by saxophonist Sam Rivers and the *nec plus ultra* for the Manhattan "loft generation." Though influenced by Archie Shepp and Albert Ayler at the start, Murray drew his true inspiration from older models, Coleman Hawkins, Sonny Rollins, and Ben Webster, pulling away from Coltrane's legacy, which made him something of an exception. He toured Europe frequently, which put him in touch with Caribbean and African musicians living in Paris. There, he grasped the relation between the different kinds of music created by the Black diaspora. "The jazz spirit enables a natural connection with all South American, Caribbean, and African music," he wrote in the liner notes to *Gwotet* (Justin Time, 2004).

As jazz artists increasingly moved toward soul and reggae, their position on issues pertaining to Black people gradually became more esthetic than political. An example was the flamboyant trumpeter Woody Shaw (no relation to Marlena), who was the traveling companion of avant-garde sax player Eric Dolphy, then member of pianist Horace Silver's quintet who would later join Art Blakey's Jazz Messengers, in 1972 and 1973. In 1969, Shaw joined the group led by Andrew Hill, a pianist of Haitian origin, for the grandiose *Lift Every Voice* (Blue Note, 1970). The record was made of five tracks with a gospel imprint, played by the quintet backed by an imposing chorale. The 2001 reissue includes six other pieces from 1970 that had remained unpublished, with Lee Morgan instead of Woody Shaw on trumpet.

In 1971, Shaw prefaced his famous *Blackstone Legacy* (Contemporary) in these terms:

This album is dedicated to the freedom of Black people. And it's dedicated to the people in the ghettos here. The 'stone' in the title is the image of strength. I grew up in a ghetto – funky houses, rats and roaches, stinking hallways. I've seen all of that, and I've seen people overcome all of that. This music is meant to be a light of hope, a sound of strength and of coming through. It's one for the ghetto.

As he grew more visible as an artist, Shaw did not deny his roots or his sense of pride in them. On his records, he repeatedly referred to the richness of Black culture. Pieces include "Soulfully I Love You (Black Spiritual of Love)" on *Love Dance* (Muse, 1976), "In the Land of the Blacks (Bilad as Sudan)", *The Woody Shaw Concert Ensemble at the Berliner Jazztage* (Muse, 1977), or "The Legend of Cheops" on the acclaimed *Rosewood* (Columbia, 1978).

Arthur Blythe also arrived in New York in 1974, and he also had roots in California. He got his start with Horace Tapscott's band on *The Giant Is Awakened* (Flying Dutchman, 1969). The sax player worked on and off with Woody Shaw and, in the process, came to be considered as a worthy heir to Coltrane. Blythe kept one foot in tradition: his 1979 album aptly entitled *In the Tradition* for Columbia was essentially a collection of standards. Meanwhile, his other foot stepped forward into the *terra incognita* of more radical experimentation, with his *Lenox Avenue Breakdown* that also came out on Columbia in 1979. No wonder Francis Davis in his book *In the Moment: Jazz in the 1980s* (Oxford University Press, 1986) considered Blythe to be "the magic figure of reconciliation, the force for con-sensus, that modern jazz has been looking for in vain since the death of John Coltrane in 1967."

At the beginning of the 1980s, the fortunes of avant-gardists like Shaw and Blythe changed with the emergence of a new generation of Black musicians who had studied at prestigious schools. A good number of them rejected, at least in appearance, the experimentation and outward expressions of militancy. They preferred to glorify a certain idea of jazz purity, understood as the fidelity to the forms and models popular before the 1970s. That meant bop and hard bop and excluded free jazz.

Since tendencies and movements need names, the music was christened "neo-bop." The New Orleans trumpeter Wynton Marsalis was touted as its quintessence, and he soon became the media's darling. And for good reason. He was a virtuoso of classical music as well as jazz, a man of erudition who never raised his voice, spoke politely of a bygone time when jazz served as a background for soirées among distinguished individuals whose class was all too apparent. He was the perfect musician for the Reagan years, the incarnation of reassuring conservativism. Consider this: he criticized artists from the libertarian avant-garde, calling them incompetent when it came to instrumental technique. At the same time, he scoffed at the ones who were seduced by the fusion with rock and other popular forms. He called them sell-outs and minstrels.

Yet Marsalis is not alienated nor assimilated. From the beginning, he displayed an awareness of the social factors that linked jazz and Black lives in America. Despite the absurd pretensions of Stanley Crouch in his liner notes, who praised the future originality of his favorite, Marsalis' album *Black Codes (From the Underground)* (Columbia, 1985) echoed a very particular period in the career of Miles Davis, the 1960s. Later, Marsalis would turn around and excoriate Davis for appearing on a number of public platforms at his disposal: it was a disgraceful act of near parricide. The album title refers both to the unwritten laws of racist repression in the Southern United States after the Civil War and the subversive strategies of resistance developed by Black people. There are other examples of Marsalis taking up the cause. Think of his ambitious trilogy *Soul Gestures in Southern Blue* with a piece dedicated to Harriet Tubman, the writer and campaigner against slavery (*Thick in the South, Vol. 1*, Columbia, 1991).

Wynton Marsalis can go ahead and accuse Miles of having become a glamorous superstar disconnected from "real" jazz and what it represents. But the latter never forgot what racism really meant, as proved by his very public run-in that left a bitter taste. I refer to the famous altercation with two New York policemen in front of the Birdland club in 1959, which ended with Miles' blood on the cops' nightsticks, and him being arrested. No wonder he joined the 1985 production of "Sun City," the protest song recorded by Artists United Against Apartheid. The list of participants was a noteworthy one, including Bob Dylan, Peter Gabriel, U2, Pat Benatar, Lou Reed, Keith Richards, Ringo Starr. Not to mention Gil Scott-Heron and George Clinton, the funk disciple of Sun Ra, and jazzmen Herbie Hancock and Ron Carter. Miles mixed humor and politics on his *Tutu* album, titling one of the pieces "Full Nelson," a reference to an old be-bop theme, "Half Nelson," as well as an homage to Nelson Mandela.

Following Wynton Marsalis, other up-and-coming young players who were prematurely and wrongly labeled "neo-bop" would dominate the 1980s and 1990s. Among them were saxophonist Branford Marsalis, Wynton's older brother, who recruited some of the greatest names in blues for a hard-hitting celebration of the first form of African American music (*I Heard You Twice the First Time*, Columbia, 1992, with B. B. King, John Lee Hooker, and other consorts). He then invited poet and militant Maya Angelou to recite her famous "I Know Why the Caged Bird Sings" over a background of jazz fusion and hip-hop on *Buckshot LeFonque* (Columbia, 1994).

A protégé of Miles associated with neo-bop and a student of Woody Shaw, trumpeter Wallace Roney created a number of pieces alluding to the struggles of African Americans. There was "Slaves" (*Verses*, Muse, 1987), "Black People Suffering" (*Seth Air*, Muse, 1991), as well as the title track of the album *No Room for Argument* (Stretch, 2001), where samples of Martin Luther King's and Malcolm X's speeches played off against a melody of percussion instruments.

Trumpeter Russell Gunn was known for his work with Branford Marsalis in the Buckshot LeFonque collective. On his own, he put out a series of six albums mixing the many forms of Black American music, from blues to hip-hop, including the different schools of jazz, represented by various labels from 1999 to 2010. He even revisited "Strange Fruit" and replied with "Stranger Fruit" on *Ethnomusicology, Vol. 3* (Justin Time, 2003).

Meanwhile, in 1997, Wynton Marsalis became the first jazz artist to win a Pulitzer Prize for composition for his *Blood on the Fields*. The piece is an indigestible and interminable oratorio for three voices and a big band and lasts more than two hours. It tells the story of two Africans, Jesse and Leona, a prince and a woman of modest origins, both sold to slave-traders and sent, along with millions of their unfortunate people, to work and die in America. For Marsalis to win such a prize for which Ellington, to name just one, was never considered created some controversy. Especially since, according to the rules, for a work to win a Pulitzer, it must be published that same year. Whereas *Blood on the Fields* was created on April 1, 1994, and issued by Columbia in 1995. Marsalis submitted "a revised version" that he had presented at Yale University in 1997 with only seven minor modifications.

Wynton went on to make *From the Plantation to the Penitentiary* (Blue Note, 2007), a virulent critique of hyper-capitalism that kept and is still keeping most African Americans second-class citizens, despite Barack Obama being elected in 2008.

∼

There are, of course, a wealth of other examples worth mentioning. Among them, I can think of the four-record set issued in spring 2012 by free jazz trumpeter Wadada Leo Smith, *Ten Freedom Summers* (Cuneiform). The album chronicles the history of the civil rights movement through its most emblematic figures, from Dred Scott to Martin Luther King, with stops at Emmett Till, Rosa Parks, Medgar Evers, and others. The work earned Smith a nomination for the Pulitzer for music in 2013.

Gil Scott-Heron predicted that the revolution would not be televised. But today's technologies have allowed people to broadcast scenes of police brutality leading to the death of Black people on YouTube and elsewhere. Take your pick. There is the case of Eric Garner, a small-time operator known to the police for trafficking in illegal cigarettes – strangled by New York policeman Daniel Pantaleo in July 2014. On the title track of his album *Breathless* (Blue Note, 2015), trumpeter Terence Blanchard, who participated with others on Spike Lee's *Malcolm X* soundtrack, brought his son, rapper and slammer JRei Oliver, into the group. His text referred not only to Garner's last words – "I can't breathe" – but also to the consequences of racism in America.

Multi-instrumentalist Marcus Miller evoked that same tragic event, and also turned to a rapper, Chuck D of Public Enemy, for "I Can't Breathe" on the album *Afrodeezia*, also a 2015 Blue Note release. Talented trumpeter Jeremy Pelt dedicated "Ruminations on Eric Garner" to the victim on *Tales, Musings and Other Reveries* (HighNote, 2015). Theo Croker, another trumpet player and the grandson of Doc Cheatham, broadened the murder into a collective symptom with his "We Can't Breathe," the featured funk and hip-hop track of his album *Escape Velocity* (Okeh, 2016). The title of another of the compositions is a complete program in itself: "A Call to the Ancestors."

Some ten years ago, composer and trumpet player Ambrose Akinmusire arrived on the scene as a band leader.

He has made government violence and systemic racism a recurring theme. On *When the Heart Emerges Glistening* (Blue Note, 2011), he refers to the case of Oscar Grant, a young Black man killed by the Oakland, California police on the first day of 2009 ("My Name Is Oscar"). The event also inspired Angie Thomas' novel *The Hate U Give*, later made into a movie by George Tillman Jr. On *The Imagined Savior Is Far Easier to Paint* (Blue Note, 2014), Akinmusire incorporates a list of Black victims of American police forces ("Rollcall for Those Absent"). On his newest album, *Origami Harvest* (Blue Note, 2018), the militant, hot-headed rapper Kool A. D. makes it clear that we have to take a position on the recurring, revolting relation between the Black community and the so-called keepers of law and order.

The return of jazz as "political" music has come thanks to the efforts of several artists, including the imposing Kamasi Washington, a tenor sax player just over 40 years old, and a key member of the flourishing Los Angeles scene. His first studio album *The Epic* (Brainfeeder, 2015) was warmly received. It praises Malcolm X, who is still controversial for his Black nationalism. "The whole point of playing this music is to convey a message," Washington declared.

It took four years of work and it runs nearly three hours; *The Epic* wears its title well. Influenced by Coltrane, the album offers a broad exploration of musical possibilities that include be-bop, modal jazz, fusion, and classical. Three years later, Washington scored again with *Heaven and Earth* (Young Turks, 2018), an album shot through with a healthy dose of Afrofuturism that would have made Sun Ra smile. On two CDs (the first concerned with earthly preoccupations, the second more spiritual), Washington and his group return to the militant 1960s and 1970s, with the hip-hop ornamentation *de rigueur* for the times.

For today's Afro-American youth, jazz may seem like academic music, middle-class, and bound to the past. Hip-hop has stepped forward as the best vehicle to express their anger at the growing racism whose believers were whipped up by a recent president. Albums like D'Angelo's *Black Messiah* (RCA, 2014) and Kendrick Lamar's *To Pimp a Butterfly* (Top Dawg, 2015), songs like "Oskar Barnack ∞ Oscar Grant" by the hip-hop duo Blue Scholars (Independent, 2011), "Hell You Talmbout" (Wondaland) by Janelle Monáe, and "Formation" (Parkwood, 2016) by Beyoncé are just a few musical examples of a renewed Black movement.

Black youth identify with these and similar pieces. Thanks to the words and the rhythms, the spirit of rebellion lives on. It is the same one that spurred on their parents and grandparents not so long ago.

BIBLIOGRAPHY

ALBERTSON, Chris : *Bessie,* Yale University Press, 1972.

ARNAUD, Noël : *Les Vies parallèles de Boris Vian,* Christian Bourgois, 1981.

BAKER, Dorothy : *Le Jeune Homme à la trompette* (translated by Boris Vian), Gallimard, 1982.

BARICCO, Alessandro : *Novecento : pianiste,* Folio, 2017.

BARICCO, Alessandro : *L'Âme de Hegel et les vaches du Wisconsin,* Folio, 2011.

BINGHAM, Dennis : *Whose Lives Are They Anyway ?: The Biopic as Contemporary Film Genre,* Rutgers, 2010.

CITRON, Stephen : *Noel and Cole: The Sophisticates,* Oxford University Press, 1993.

CLARKE, Donald : *Wishing on the Moon: The Life and Times of Billie Holiday,* Viking Penguin, 1994.

DAVIS, Miles : *Miles, l'autobiographie* (with the collaboration of Quincy Troupe, translation by Christian Gauffre, preface by Pierre-Jean Crittin), Gollion, 2007.

DONALD, James : *Some of These Days: Black Stars, Jazz Aesthetics, and Modernist Culture,* Oxford University Press, 2015.

DYER, Geoff : *Jazz impro,* translated by Rémy Lambrechts, Paris, Éditions 10/18, coll. « Musiques & cie », 2002.

FAIRWEATHER, Digby : *The Oxford Companion to Jazz,* Oxford University Press, 2000.

GAILLY, Christian : *Be-bop,* Éditions de Minuit, 1995.

GAILLY, Christian : *Un soir au club,* Éditions de Minuit, 2002.

GAVIN, James : *Deep in a Dream: The Long Night of Chet Baker,* Chicago Review Press, 2002.

GILLESPIE, Dizzy : *To Bop or Not to Bop,* Doubleday, 1979.

GIOA, Ted : *The History of Jazz,* Oxford University Press, 2011.

GOLDSHER, Alan : *Hard Bop Academy: The Sidemen of Art Blakey and the Jazz Messenger,* Hal Leonard, 2003.

GREEN, Benny : *The Reluctant Art: Five Studies in the Growth of Jazz,* Da Capo Press, 1962.

HODEIR, André : *Hommes et problèmes du jazz,* Parenthèses, 1981

LION, Jean-Pierre : *Bix Beiderbecke, une biographie,* Outre Mesure, 2004.

LYNSKEY, Dorian : *33 Revolutions per Minute: A History of Protest Songs, from Billie Holiday to Green Day,* Harper Collins, 2011.

MARGOLICK, David : *Strange Fruit: Billie Holiday, Café Society, and an Early Cry for Civil Rights,* Running Press, 2000.

McBRIEN, William : *Cole Porter: A Biography,* Knopf, 1998.

McMILLAN, Jeffrey S. : *DelightfulLee: The Life and Music of Lee Morgan,* University of Michigan Press, 2008.

NICHOLSON, Stuart : *Billie Holiday,* North Eastern University Press, 1995.

PERCHARD, Tom : *Lee Morgan: His Life, Music and Culture,* Equinox, 2006.

POUCHKINE, Alexandre : *Mozart et Salieri* (translation from Russian, foreword and afterword by Jean-Pierre Pisetta), Éditions Bernard Gilson, 2006.

RAMEY, Doug : *Jazz Matters: Reflections on the Music and Some of Its Makers,* University of Arkansas Press, 1989.

REISNER, Bob : *Bird : The Legend of Charlie Parker,* Da Capo Press, 1977.

ROBERT, Danièle : *Les Chants de l'aube de Lady Day,* Triptyque, 2002.

SAGAN, Françoise : *Avec mon meilleur souvenir,* Gallimard, 1984.

SARTRE, Jean-Paul : *La Nausée,* Gallimard, 1938.

SEITÉ, Yannick : *Le Jazz à la lettre : la littérature et le jazz,* Presses universitaires de France, coll. « Les littéraires », 2010.